making

JOB SHARING MIH
TWO HEADS ARE BETTER THAN ONE

Also available in this series:

making it happen

JOB SHARING MIH
TWO HEADS ARE BETTER THAN ONE

**ANGELA MORELLA
AND MARY O'HANLON**

ALLEN&UNWIN

First published in 2003

Allen & Unwin
83 Alexander Street
Crows Nest NSW 2065
Australia

Phone: (61 2) 8425 0100
Fax: (61 2) 9906 2218
Email: info@allenandunwin.com
Web: www.allenandunwin.com

National Library of Australia
Cataloguing-in-Publication entry:

O'Hanlon, Mary, 1960– .
Job sharing: two heads are better than one.

Bibliography.
Includes index.
ISBN 1 86508 964 8.

1. Job sharing. 2. Work sharing. 3. Part-time employment.
I. Morella, Angela, 1960– . II. Title. (Series: Making
it happen).

331.2572

Set in 11.5/14 pt Bembo by Midland Typesetters, Maryborough, Victoria
Printed in Australia by McPherson's Printing Group

10 9 8 7 6 5 4 3 2 1

about

the series

making it happen

Are you committed to changing things for the better? Are you searching for ways to make your organisation more effective? Are you trying to help your people and organisation to improve, but are seriously strapped for time and money? If you are, then this Making It Happen book is written specifically for you.

Every book in the series is designed to assist change agents to get things done . . . to make new programs really happen . . . without costing the organisation an arm and a leg and without taking up all of your valuable time.

Each book in the series is written by a top consultant in the field who does not simply theorise about their subject of expertise but who explains specifically how to implement a program that will really work for your unit or organisation. Vital advice on what works and what doesn't work, what tricks to use and traps to avoid, plus suggested strategies for implementation, templates and material to photocopy, and checklists to gauge your readiness — each book in the series is filled with useful information, all written in clear, practical language that enables you to make things happen, fast.

Help your people and work unit to increase their performance and love their work through implementing a program from the Making It Happen series and reap the rewards that successful change agents deserve.

about
the book

Job sharing is one of many flexible work practices available today. Highly rewarding yet not without its own unique difficulties and challenges, job sharing is being adopted by more and more people and companies as a viable alternative to more conventional full-time positions. It's a win–win situation — by offering more flexible arrangements, both you and your employer will reap the benefits of increased productivity and heightened motivation.

If you're looking for a better balance in your life, or a change in the way you manage your career and family life, then job sharing might be a solution that could work for you. This book takes you through the steps to:

- find out if job sharing will suit you
- find a compatible job-share partner who is just as hardworking and reliable as you are
- prepare a persuasive proposal to convince your boss of the benefits of job sharing
- learn how to deal with the day-to-day challenges of sharing a position.

Job Sharing: Two heads are better than one offers you all the information, strategies and confidence you need to negotiate the work-life balance you're looking for, including:

- activities to help you assess what you want from your life, and to understand the types of flexibility you may need
- a look inside some workplaces that support job sharing, and how they do it
- case studies of successful individuals and organisations.

Designed to give practical ideas on how to go about job sharing in the workplace, this book tackles the difficulties and challenges of working outside a typical work situation while continuing to deliver quality outcomes. You will find suggestions on how to manage yourself, your job-share partner, your boss, your colleagues, your co-workers and those you supervise. Job sharing is not for the faint hearted — but this book shows you how, with a little preparation and forethought, work can be successfully delivered and outcomes achieved.

Whether you're at the top of the corporate ladder, just starting out, thinking of returning to the workforce after a break, or moving towards retirement, job sharing can provide you with the balance you want in your work and personal life. This book will show you how to make the vision of creating a balanced life a reality.

about
the authors

Angela Morella has built a successful career, spanning some 20 years, spotting and seizing opportunities. These opportunities, ranging from contract and project management to strategic business planning, marketing and communications, opened up numerous challenges which broadened her skills and experiences.

Angela is married to Paul and they have a daughter Isabella. She has a Bachelor of Arts degree in psychology and languages from the Australian National University. During her studies, Angela learnt her first important lessons in how to balance different life priorities — she completed her degree while working full time.

Angela lives her life guided by the belief that it is important to seek out and build upon the best of life's opportunities. These include relationships with loved ones, the blessings received from nurturing and watching a child grow and the excitement of a challenging career. In order to do this, Angela believes one needs to cultivate balance.

Mary O'Hanlon is a former athlete who achieved success in netball at the Australian Institute of Sport. Her mission in life is to make a contribution to all who are seeking more balance in their lives and who believe there is a better way of doing things. Mary is a passionate believer in striving to do the best one can in all aspects of life. Mary worked part time as a sales assistant while she studied Applied Science at the University of Western Melbourne. Following this she worked for three years as Coaching Director for Netball in the ACT. Her public sector experience also includes stints in printing and publishing, corporate management, strategic planning and experience in a number of government businesses. She currently leads a team in the national product and service development unit of her organisation.

One of Mary's keen areas of interest is recognising the potential in an integrated life. She is very aware of the third job syndrome — work, parenting and house — 'and that it doesn't allow for a relationship, let alone time for exploring one's self,' she adds. Part of her reasons for writing this book is to explore how to thrive while being aware of one's potential in a number of areas.

Mary is married to Garry, who works part time as a computer analyst. Together they share the parenting responsibilities for their two children, Catherine and James.

acknowledgements

In writing a book which focuses on our personal work experiences over a number of years, it is difficult to single out individuals for acknowledgement. Thank you to those people whose open minds and creative thinking allowed us to try job share in the first place. We have used many of your stories, or an amalgam of them, in this publication.

Thank you to our publishers for all the effort put in.

Our friends have provided us with encouragement and practical suggestions. These have buoyed us beyond measure. Thank you.

Our families, those living near and far, have been wonderfully supportive. Our husbands and children are the reason we looked for flexible approaches to our work. In a very real way we are all in this together!

Angela and Mary

contents

Why job share?

- The value of job sharing

- Job sharing does work

- Benefits for the organisation

- Benefits for the individual

- Trends for job sharing

- Some points to ponder

The vision is to build a balanced life through flexible work and career opportunities.

Globalisation and the demands for 24-hour service at less cost have accelerated the rate of change in our workplaces. It is becoming increasingly recognised by governments and organisations the world over that there are significant benefits for both employers and employees in considering work–life balance.

Why is this so? Why are companies — profit focused as they are — considering the value of improved working arrangements for employees?

The answer lies partly in the evolution of employment as a social characteristic: we care more about how we work and the culture in which we work. Perhaps more important, however, is the rapidly changing dynamics of business — companies have to be more creative, flexible and responsive to survive. One way to increase corporate dynamism is to create an environment that automatically engenders these values in employees. The recognition of this gives employment practices, such as flexible working arrangements, a focus and relevance that may not have existed otherwise.

■ THE VALUE OF JOB SHARING

The need to balance the personal interests of its employees with the interests of the organisation is a critical measure of a company's success. Not only are a company's employment policies a significant contributor to their corporate profile, company results are increasingly dependent upon successful and innovative employment strategies. In today's global marketplace, organisations need to be able to attract and retain staff while maintaining leadership in a competitive field.

Charles Handy recognised this in his most recent book, *The Elephant and the Flea*:

> *Already research is establishing that . . . flexible working and job sharing, the latter mostly used by women, are resulting in improved productivity and job satisfaction. BT in Britain views flexible working as important to the retention of talent in some of their divisions.*

Others also point to returns gained through flexible employment strategies:[1]

> *Finalists and winners in the Work and Family Awards[2] regularly comment that there are significant reductions in absenteeism, and improved job satisfaction. They also comment that they have attracted larger, more diverse and talented fields of job applicants.*

There is a widely held view that companies will move towards more open, networked structures and project-based modes of operation. This allows greater flexibility, a focus on results and minimises the risks to shareholders of new ventures not working. This approach is already well established in creative industries, such as film and media, service industries, such as tourism and hospitality, and is increasingly applied in the tele-communications and information technology sectors.

A useful concept to apply this approach to more traditional industries is that of 'value creation'. Karl Albrecht, who contributed to moving management thinking from Total Quality Management to Total Quality Service in the late 1980s and early 1990s, said that in order to create intrinsic value, organisations needed to adopt 'a business philo-sophy, a form of leadership, a collective spirit of service, and a new way of operating that embraces quality and customer value as its guiding principle'.

Value creation can sometimes be difficult to define in simple, everyday language. An analogy of a symphony orchestra captures the intent of this sometimes elusive concept: many of us have experienced the magic and emotion that an excellent piece of music performed by an exceptional orchestra can create — when the music makes the hair on the back of your neck stand up — that's value creation. A good conductor (manager) knows how to bring together the bits of music and the many different instruments beyond the mere notes on the page to create that value.

We firmly believe that employers who strive for value creation for their customers need to internalise the concept to create value for their employees. To create the best value options for clients, employers need to increasingly think laterally about staff selection, skilling and support.

It's no longer just about covering the hours and producing a set of outputs. It's about creating a valued outcome for the customer. This, therefore, needs to be paralleled with a fresh approach to role and work outcome definitions. It forces employers to be clear about the outcome rather than focus on the processes alone.

It's about matching jobs to client needs — hours become a somewhat secondary consideration. The hours worked is only one part of the equation and this needs to be considered on par with the value creation concept. Similar to Albrecht's concept of 'quality and customer value', internal organisational value creation must stem from a strong leadership and cultural platform which supports this concept.

■ JOB SHARING DOES WORK

Flexible working arrangements, such as part time and job sharing, increasingly succeed at a senior level. The research group Catalyst in the United States has tracked 24 women who first used flexible working arrangements more than ten years ago. The findings of this study are quite interesting — not only have more than half of the women earned promotions in the past decade, all of them now hold mid- and senior-level positions. Half still maintain part-time hours and half have returned to full-time work.

Both of us are living, breathing examples of the same principles at work. But don't just take our word for it. There are a number of companies who, through their family friendly work practices, are offering flexible working arrangements including job sharing, and who are reaping the benefits of doing so.

The Commonwealth Bank Group has a long history of flexible and family friendly work practices. They introduced part-time employment in 1967 and paid parental leave in 1973. In 1990, the Bank introduced a range of flexible work practices including a job-share scheme. As at September 2001, there were just under 800 employees job sharing. The Bank summarises the benefits of its job-share scheme as follows. There is:

- always someone in the job for colleagues, supervisors and managers who need information or assistance
- maintenance and enhancement of employee skill levels which benefits both the employer and the employee
- a reduction in absenteeism and turnover which leads to a reduction in recruitment and training costs
- higher morale and higher productivity
- higher retention of employees following maternity leave
- generally less childcare costs when working in a job–share arrangement than a part–time arrangement.

Alcoa World Alumina Australia introduced a number of family friendly initiatives in recent years, including flexible work options involving job share. Some of their goals have been to stimulate employee commitment to the business and its performance, and to develop higher levels of trust, mutual understanding and teamwork between all employees. Their President, Mike Baltezell, is quoted as saying:

When an individual's work and family lives are in balance, they come to work in a more positive frame of mind. They are safer, more productive employees and they go home more satisfied people.[3]

SC Johnson — a family owned, fast moving, consumer goods company — measures the outcomes of its work–life balance program. This program includes flexible working arrangements such as job share. The results indicate improved employee retention, overall employee satisfaction and increased pride and commitment with a reduction in recruitment costs.[4]

As you can see, job sharing is now becoming more recognised as a vehicle for introducing flexibility in jobs that require a 'full-time presence'. People from all avenues of work, such as professionals — for example, teachers and health workers — as well as clerical, administrative and managerial positions, are looking for the ability to balance life's demands through job sharing. So the possibilities are there for all of us.

■ BENEFITS FOR THE ORGANISATION

'We have traditionally fitted the people to the work, now we may have to fit the work to the people, as they become our key assets.' — Charles Handy

There are many potential benefits to organisations as a result of being open to job sharing. Initially we shall focus on just two:
- improved productivity
- reduced staff turnover.

A full list of potential benefits is outlined at the end of this chapter.

Anecdotally, improved productivity is often listed as a benefit of part-time and job-sharing arrangements. A recent study, however, attempted to quantify this. A study presented at the British Psychological Society's occupational psychology conference in January 2001 claimed that managers who cut down their hours or work from home are out-performing those who put in a traditional nine-to-five workday. 'A survey of almost 200 people in senior jobs with flexible working arrangements, such as job-shares or reduced hours, found that 70% had a 30% higher level of output and scored higher on resilience, leadership and commitment than their traditional full time colleagues.'[5]

It seems ironic that reduced hours can lead to increased productivity. The logical thought is that because there is less time, less will be achieved. However, sometimes the reverse is true. Because there is less time available to complete the work, a greater effort is made to complete the work in the available time. As one worker in Juliet Bourke's study 'Corporate Women, Children, Careers and Workplace Culture' said:

Being able to work part time has (I think) . . . helped me to be more organised, focused and efficient at work largely because I know I can only devote so much of my time to the role.

Our own experience supports this.

We were very aware that we were undertaking a workload that was far greater than one individual could manage in our job-share partnership. Our focus was greater because we wanted both the job and the way we were undertaking the job to succeed. Feedback from our supervisor was also quite positive in this regard. We were each considered to have a substantial workload as individuals and as a team and still produced quality work.

Reducing staff turnover is another significant organisational benefit. In December 1999, the Commonwealth Bank in Australia undertook a survey of staff involved in job sharing. When asked if they would have resigned if they could not job share, 27.4 per cent said 'definitely, yes', 40.4 per cent said 'probably', 19.8 per cent were unsure and 10.5 per cent said 'unlikely'. Only 1.9 per cent said they would definitely not have resigned.

The Evening Standard in London reported in July 2001 that talent and skill shortage is considered by many managers to be one of the biggest issues currently facing business, and offering flexibility has been shown to help with employee retention. Sun Micro-systems recently revealed that after the introduction of flexible working practices two years ago it has reduced its staff turnover and boosted employee satisfaction. When flexible working was introduced the company staff turnover stood around 10 per cent — it is now at almost zero and three-quarters of the workforce report being happy with the changes.[6]

A surprising organisational benefit may be protecting the company from possible legal challenges. Two recent tribunal cases considered indirect sex discrimination for women with family responsibilities. In both cases employees were seeking to work on a job-share or part-time basis and both requests had been rejected by the employer. The tribunals found in favour of the employees. In one case, the tribunal listed the potential benefits of job sharing to be 'increased flexibility, retention of qualified and experienced staff, probably lower rates of absenteeism and sick leave (to mention a few)'. (Juliet Bourke)

Therefore the potential benefits of job sharing include staff retention, reduction in staff turnover, improved morale, increased work coverage and lower absenteeism. In our view the advantages of job sharing far outweigh any disadvantages. It is true that an organisation may need to consider work patterns other than nine to five and that super-visors need to consider two staff members where previously they had to consider only one (we give some hints on how to do this in Chapter 6), but taking the bigger picture into account, staff and employees can both win.

■ BENEFITS FOR THE INDIVIDUAL

With more than a quarter of the workforce in most developed countries working part time there is a large body of knowledge about the health and well-being of part time workers.

A recent analysis of Australian workplaces drew two relevant conclusions. First, flexible hours are the most popular family friendly provision and, second, employees are more likely to have better satisfaction and experience less stress if they are able to work their preferred weekly hours and use time flexibly at work.[7] It is just a small step to see how employees who are more satisfied and less stressed give better return to the workplace.

Job sharing has some specific individual benefits. Apart from the obvious increased flexibility, job sharing provides specific benefits such as:[8]

- the sense of legitimacy and other benefits that come with working in a full-time job, albeit in a part-time capacity
- the possibility of a partnership where one's skills and abilities are complemented by the other partner
- opportunities to learn from the job-sharing partner
- mutual support and encouragement on the job.

We found job sharing important for a number of reasons, including those outlined above. Primarily, though, job sharing helped us integrate the various aspects of our lives — we could continue our working career, home career, work in the community as well as renovate houses, write a book and so on. Job sharing reduced the amount of conflict between the various areas of our lives and enabled us to establish legitimacy in the work-place. Our working lives have always been important to us, but so are other areas of our lives.

We are not the only people who have made flexible working arrangements succeed at a senior level. Initially, the impetus for legal firm Blake Dawson and Waldron to intro-duce a family-friendly environment was to retain valued female lawyers with family commitments. Soon it became obvious that work–life balance was an issue for many staff. Blake Dawson and Waldron have implemented a number of policies, such as flexible hours — including part time and casual — various forms of leave and access to laptops and home offices. Currently about ten per cent of partners and staff work part time (including five partners). Part of the shift in their culture was to see flexible arrangements as a natural part of the career path, not a career obstacle. (Elizabeth Broderick)

It is important to recognise, however, that many people choose to work full time. A survey found that a quarter of those questioned worked part time (DEWR 1995). However, the same survey indicated that 61 per cent of people felt they could work part time if they wanted. Clearly, more people still prefer to work full time than not.

There are some obvious costs to the individual engaged in part-time as opposed to full-time work. These include:

- reduced income
- potential confusion over conditions and entitlements
- reduced profile in the workplace.

These disadvantages are well known but widely accepted. In fact, for the vast majority of women in many countries they are a normal condition of employment. In Australia, for example, over a quarter of the workforce works part time and 73 per cent of all part-time employees are women. Only 13 per cent of all employed men are part time compared to 44 per cent of women. (DEWR 2001)

It is important not to over-emphasise the similarities between part-time employment and job sharing. In addition to the disincentives for part-time work, implementing a job-sharing project offers different challenges to those of a part-time position. It is one of the objectives of this book to show how these challenges can be overcome and the benefits achieved.

■ TRENDS FOR JOB SHARING

If we stand back and look at human society as a whole over the period of several centuries, work practices have been in a state of change since the Industrial Revolution. Whereas most workers prior to the rise of the modern city were relatively independent in their day-to-day activities and worked more or less to their own rhythms, they had almost no control over the nature or conditions of their employment and reward for their labour.

The centralisation of manufacturing and commerce gave rise to the modern notion of the worker and, in turn, the rise of the notion of rights and conditions of employment. For a variety of reasons, centralisation appears to have peaked and we are now experiencing a long-term trend toward more flexible work practices. In developed countries this translates directly to a rise in job sharing.

The desire to implement flexible work arrangements such as job sharing is a global phenomenon. It is part of best practice the world over.

The UK government launched a work–life balance campaign in 2000. In addition, an alliance of UK business leaders formed 'Employers for Work–Life Balance'. The European Union established the European Foundation for the Improvement of Living and Work Conditions as far back as May 1975.

In 1999, the US Department of Labor assembled a comprehensive view of the world of work called 'Futurework: trends and challenges for work in the 21st century'. Many Swedish organisations have tried paying employees for a seven- or eight-hour day while they only work six.

Perhaps Graham Russell and Lyndy Bowmann summarise the world picture best in FaCS 2000:[9]

It is evident that analyses conducted in several countries reveal a common pattern in the recent shifts in approaches to work and family. First, there has been a shift from a narrow focus on work and family to an acceptance that work, family, personal and community commitments all need to be considered.

In Australia the *Workplace Relations Act* in 1996 centred around providing choice for both employees and employers on how they deal with their workplace relations. The principle objective includes 'assisting employees to balance their work and family responsibilities effectively through the development of mutually beneficial work practices with employers'. (DEWR 1998) At about the same time, the Work and Family Unit in the Department of Employment, Workplace Relations and Small Business (DEWRSB) was set up. The unit's role is to advise on policy issues relating to work and family and to implement strategies aimed at improving work–life balance. This includes commissioning research into the Australian workforce, co-sponsoring the Australian Chamber of Commerce and Industry (ACCI) Corporate Work and Family Awards as well as providing guidelines for employers on workplace issues. The Work and Family Unit provides a series of resource tools aimed largely at employers and Human Resource professionals, as well as guidance on establishing work and family policies and programs.

Elizabeth Hall, in her New Zealand study of job sharing (1993), concluded that although in the past job sharing was driven by employees it is now being seen by both employers and employees as providing significant advantages in flexibility, skills maintenance and recruitment.

HOW DOES JOB SHARING WORK IN PRACTICE? — ONE BOSS'S VIEWPOINT
Below are a few grabs from an interview we did with a CEO we have worked with in a job-sharing arrangement. It covers the key points of what the organisation gets, potential pitfalls, and perceived limitations of job sharing as an employment practice. The CEO's words are in italics.

The organisation has clearly got more than a full-time job equivalent. There is no doubt about that.

The primary benefit has two main aspects. First, the richer contribution that a team makes than an individual. This should also open our minds to replacing two positions with three people, setting up project teams and other arrangements that none of us may have thought of yet. Second, the productivity of people who work less than full time. We could all learn something here — about our personal work ethic, and about being focused and using time wisely to complete the job at hand.

To get the best for the organisation, you need to accept and acknowledge that people have other elements to their lives that they need to balance.

The secondary benefit to the organisation comes from having happy employees. Clearly, the benefit is not direct since the organisation *needs to accept* the benefits to the individual. Nevertheless, this is a net benefit to the organisation.

The negatives were about not being able to talk to the person that I wanted to talk to. I recognise that this situation can apply regardless of the nature of the working relationship. I sometimes can't get to people who are here full time either.

This negative, as acknowledged, may exist in environments with no job sharing. However, in a job-sharing environment it is clearly going to be seen as a result of the change in work practices. This is not simply a matter of perception, however. Unless the potential for these problems is closely managed the real benefits will be undermined. Like most jobs, job sharing involves managing the dynamics in the workplace as well as the job itself.

In a larger, ongoing operational management role with significant numbers of staff where your primary job is about leadership, it would not work even in a job-share arrangement. It creates ambiguity.

Even in an enlightened organisation with encouraging management and enthusiastic employees there is a glass ceiling or, at the very least, a *type* of job at which job-sharing arrangements are likely to cause problems. It is our personal belief that this comment may be proven wrong over time and we may see CEOs of major corporations shying away from the high-power, high-pressure profile that we associate with those positions.

Until that becomes reality, though, we have to live with the fact that job sharing has not been successfully implemented in executive positions in major companies. The absence of women from work while child-rearing is the most quoted reason for their absence in the ranks of upper management.

■ SOME POINTS TO PONDER

What is your current organisation like? Are there many staff who work hours other than the standard 9 a.m. to 5 p.m.? What is the diversity of senior managers in your workplace? Are they typically of one gender? With one dominant lifestyle? Is change accepted in your organisation? Does much change happen at all? If you answered no to any of these questions you may like to consider the thoughts below.

If you are brave and there is some management support, job sharing at a senior level can provide a great opportunity to drive change within such an organisation. Our experience is that it can loosen up traditional ways of thinking and can certainly move people out of their comfort zones — both the job sharers and other staff in the organisation!

> Sometimes an organisation can experience a whole new set of freedoms simply by having someone undertake work in a different way.

Just a word of caution here before you set out to change the world. Make sure you have some organisational support. It takes enough effort to make job sharing work in a reasonably positive environment, let alone one where there is considerable resistance. This book is all about setting you up to succeed — not to fail!

■ SUMMARY

Flexible work practices allow organisations to employ individuals in configurations that may not otherwise be possible. The large percentage of women who work part time attests to this. Just as the workplace would be poorer for the absence of those part-time workers, so it can benefit from extending the flexibility of the arrangements for other workers.

The enthusiasm of workers for these arrangements has encouraged governments around the world to introduce legislation or regulations that enshrine the right of workers to flexibility in their conditions of employment. The benefits to the organisation go beyond the legal environment established by these moves, however.

- Two part-time workers often contribute more than one full-time employee. Except for process-related work, the organisation has two minds applying themselves to the one task that will often result in better solutions.
- The fact that two people are sharing a job means they have to organise themselves, take note of where they are up to and what has to be delivered, and communicate that to each other. This process can lead to more efficient work practices and a better interface with the rest of the organisation. Of course, if these things do not happen, neither do these benefits to the organisation.
- One of the major potential benefits for an organisation in moving to flexible work practices is that it mirrors the kind of flexible relationships that increasingly dominate business. Companies compete at some levels and cooperate at others. Companies form short-term relationships with individuals on a business-to-business basis. By exploring the organisational issues inherent in job sharing, companies can open themselves up to new means of operating in these environments.
- Employees who engage in flexible work practices to better balance their personal and work lives will be happier. Happy employees are loyal employees and keep down the costs associated with staff turnover, recruitment and training.

chapter 2

Know your organisation

- Should an organisation consider job sharing?

- For which type of organisation does job sharing work?

- Can your organisation support job sharing?

In Chapter 1 we outlined some of the benefits for an organisation considering job sharing. However, a simple pros and cons argument is not enough for an organisation to take on a job-sharing option. Flexible work practices may not benefit every industry.

It is a reality that some industries, which could potentially benefit from them, will not be able to implement the principles discussed in this book because of entrenched cultures or external circumstances that resist them. The nature of the work may require long periods of time away from home base (e.g. welders on deep sea oil rigs, pilots, defence forces personnel, maintenance workers in industries such as railway or telecommunications) and it is difficult to see how job share could work in such environments.

> **Understanding the nature of your organisation is critical to determining how, and indeed if, you can implement job sharing.**

■ SHOULD AN ORGANISATION CONSIDER JOB SHARING?

Organisations are a lot like people — they have tangible structures that support and sustain activity and a less tangible psyche that contributes to its uniqueness. It is these tangible and intangible elements that can provide a clue as to whether an organisation is able to consider job sharing and whether you should consider putting a job-sharing proposal to them.

The tangible structures include physical parameters such as the:
- number of employees
- number of offices
- geographic location
- corporate or political structure
- reporting requirements
- major mechanisms for dealing with customers or clients.

In addition to this physical environment there are many issues regarding the nature of the business that will influence how the business operates. These include:
- operating hours
- type and range of customers
- the different ways of dealing with customers (face-to-face, phone, Internet, written)
- peak hours and seasonal periods.

There are issues relating to the culture of the organisation — the regulatory framework; the policies that have been adopted and implemented by management; the historical involvement of unions; the profile of the workforce to name a few. Although these relate to the culture within the organisation they are still tangible.

The intangible elements are sometimes harder to define and are based on the 'feel' of an organisation. This 'feel' can rely on aspects such as the:

- personality of the CEO
- personalities of the leadership team
- stated organisational values (if any)
- examples of where these values have been actively 'lived' (how people behave as opposed to lip service).

They are intangible because they may not always be obvious or written down. They are also much harder to find out about. However, the intangible elements are critical to determining whether flexible work practices will actually be feasible as it is easier to write a policy allowing job sharing than to actually implement it.

These tangible and intangible aspects provide a framework for understanding your organisation and some insight into where it might be coming from in terms of it being able to consider flexible work practices such as job sharing. Let's now look at the key indicators of whether your organisation might be able to adopt job-sharing practices. The worksheets in Chapter 6 can be used to work through this process and help you draw your own conclusion about how you might approach implementing such a scheme.

FLEXIBLE AND INFLEXIBLE ORGANISATIONS

Truly flexible organisations can possibly be defined as those where the tangible (policies) and the intangible (the way the organisation lives out its policies) are aligned. These organisations seem to be charged with a great deal of positive energy. This energy is in part directed at providing the best possible work environment for their employees, recognising that with this support, their employees are better positioned to deliver the best outcomes. These organisations:

- are open to innovative approaches
- appear to have the 'space' and willingness to experiment
- are prepared to invest more generously in staff development and support.

The atmosphere and the culture generated by a flexible organisation appear to provide the type of support that is needed to create and sustain innovative approaches to work. In short, these organisations are the ones most often referred to as 'family friendly'. Some of the winning strategies used by flexible organisations include:

- flexible start and finish times
- the ability to work a preferred number of hours per week
- work–life balanced weeks
- graduated retirement plan
- the ability to leave work without penalty to attend to personal responsibilities.

Flexible organisations are responding to the fact that more and more people are looking for and demanding flexibility in their working lives. Flexible organisations, recognising this, are being driven not just by the need to retain good staff but also the desire to attract quality new employees. Employers want to be seen as the employer of choice to attract good staff.

As mentioned in Chapter 1, it also makes good economic sense for organisations to be seen to be at the leading edge of developments for employees. Quality organisations are investing significant resources in developing and maintaining the professionalism and expertise of their people. These investments are in the form of recruitment, training, skills upgrading, improving industry and technical knowledge and personal development. It's in their best interest then to create environments that retain staff so that they can make the most of these investments.

Our experience has taught us that there are a number of clues which point to the readiness of an organisation to accept or support flexible work choices. The tangible can be done by pursuing the organisation's policies in relation to their workers and the working conditions (you will need to find a copy of these — try human resources departments). Some aspects to look for include a strong people commitment reflected in corporate documentation and outlined in employment conditions, and explicit acknowledgment of the need for work–life balance and flexibility in the workplace. There is a detailed checklist in Chapter 6 (Activity 1, Worksheet 1) which provides more ideas on what to look for.

Seeking the intangible elements may take more work. We have found that whilst an organisation may have all the right policies in place (tangible aspects) they may only pay them lip service in reality (intangible aspects). We suggest seeking out the actual usage of any existing work provisions — the behaviours of the leadership team and other key decision makers in the organisation and evidence of organisational values being 'lived out'. The questions in Activity 1, Worksheet 2 help you discern the intangible elements of a flexible organisation.

It is important to see through any lip service.

We have been part of organisations undergoing downsizing and have observed a number of others that were also undergoing major change. It struck us that organisations which were struggling to maintain market or industry positioning were quite different to flexible organisations. Their state of flux led to a more rigid approach to work activity — almost a 'bunkering down' mentality. It appeared that they had 'less space' to allow for difference. This may not be the best type of organisation (or employer) that would support flexibility in its workplace. As an employee of such an organisation you need to look for the tangible and intangible clues on how the organisation is responding to its downsizing environment, and then determine how you want to approach flexible work.

However, we did not think it helpful to think of organisations as simply either having flexibility or not having flexibility. In our experience it is simply not that black and white — organisations are often a mixture of both. In order to help with this type of thinking we developed a worksheet (Chapter 6, Activity 1, Worksheet 3) which may help you to place your organisation on the continuum of more to less flexible.

We have encountered CEOs with a wide range of views and experiences. In the interest of ensuring we provide you with balance it is worth spending a little time on this issue as well. We worked at one stage in an organisation that was facing a significant crisis. This included a significant restructure with the subsequent downsizing of over two-thirds of its staff. The General Manager at the time suggested to us that he couldn't 'afford the luxury of job sharing'.

To date, we have had six different managers in three organisations, both as part timers and job sharers. On the whole, most of the managers have been supportive of the concept of flexible work options. However, each of these managers has taken a different approach to both part-time work and job sharing. These approaches reflected a blend of their beliefs and those of the organisation.

At the end of the day, to be successful in flexible employment we need to be able to decipher both the tangible and intangible aspects of the organisation. This is no small task. The tools provided in Activity 1 will help you do this. They will provide strong clues as to whether your organisation should consider job-sharing arrangements and, if so, how to position your job-sharing proposal (see Activity 10 for a practical application of this). But of course, that is not the end of the story.

■ FOR WHICH TYPE OF ORGANISATION DOES JOB SHARING WORK?

This is a question we often get asked. We are as surprised as anyone to find that job sharing exists in a range of industries across a range of levels and within all sectors. This section will provide some examples of where job sharing has been successful.

PRIVATE VS PUBLIC SECTOR

The public sector, being closer to government policy, has tended to lead the way in implementing the regulation referred to in trends for job sharing (Chapter 1). This complements, however, the trend in the private sector for outsourcing, contracting and flatter management structures. The major difference between the two is that the public sector tends to be driven by political considerations whereas the private sector is driven by the bottom line. By understanding the outcomes of implementing such programs across the board we can better meet the needs of both the individual and the workplace. Because programs implemented in large corporations have tended to focus on profitability, studying them exposes the principles that protect the organisation and reveals some of the pitfalls for individuals. The reverse is possibly true of the public sector.

Some examples

We successfully job shared a senior position in the business development unit of a federal government agency for over five years. Responsible for strategic planning, communication, evaluation of client satisfaction and review of the client charter, we played a key role in the organisation's change agenda. We managed a small team and worked to integrate our personal and professional lives. The case study at the end of this chapter mentions the benefits gained by our organisation.

The Ford Motor Company of Australia's two key job-sharing successes are in the reception area and a personal assistant's role, which has been job shared for some time. They have also had other instances where people have opted to job share for defined periods of time. The arrangements are so successful in one case that some people appear to have missed the fact that there are two people in the job! Ford sees flexible work options as another way to attract and retain talent, improve productivity, promote diversity and work–life balance and improve the Ford brand.

Private sector workplaces (with 20 or more employees) account for 71 per cent (AWIRS 1995) of all workplaces. It could be said that in some ways both public and private sectors are becoming more alike. The call for the private sector to consider the 'third bottom line' in terms of community values and ecological considerations has caused it to become somewhat akin to the public sector. With these changes, flexible work practices can work in both sectors.

The changing nature of the public sector with its shrinking resources, outsourcing and service demands has made it more and more aligned to the private sector.

Having worked in both commercial and non-commercial organisations, we believe that flexible work practices can work in both sectors and across different size organisations. Biggs and Fallon Horgan's *Time on, Time Out!* book refers to a number of private sector organisations that have active flexible employment policies and programs.

COMMUNITY AND CORPORATE

Organisations which provide direct care to clients in the community also have successful job-share arrangements. Family Based Care Association (North Inc.) is a community-based aged and disability service delivery organisation in the northern region of Tasmania in Australia and has over 220 staff. Job sharing provides benefits for the direct care workers (those who work directly with the client in their home) by reducing workplace stress and burnout. Clients also benefit by having a variety of people to interact with (which is particularly important for housebound clients). Health care coordinators are another high stress role which uses job sharing to alleviate burnout. In this case, the client benefits by having different workers with a different perspective on the same issue and therefore different solutions.

Companies such as Hewlett-Packard Australia Limited (HP) see the benefit of flexible work arrangements. This company provides computing and imaging solutions and services around the world. They see work–life balance as important in keeping employees fresh and renewed, and it is something that HP works hard at achieving. Job sharing is one arrangement used by the company to promote a flexible, supportive environment to manage work and personal life demands. At HP, job sharing occurs within the sales area, providing administrative support to two different managers and their respective teams. For the employees, job sharing allows the desire and energy to combine both family and work commitments. HP believes that one key to employee loyalty is to balance productive work against lifestyle needs.

LARGE AND SMALL

BTR Automotive Drivetrain Systems is an automotive transmission manufacturer based in Albury, New South Wales, Australia. They are a large organisation with over 800 staff. Currently, job-sharing positions have been taken up by factory (both male and female staff), clerical and nursing staff. The main benefit to the organisation is that they have afforded flexibility and coverage — if one staff member is away the other will cover. Benefits for the employees are seen as greater flexibility, shorter hours and more leisure time. BTR Automotive has also introduced an optional part-time schedule for night shift employees, reducing the work hours from 8 to 6.5.

When we thought about small businesses we realised that many business partnerships may in fact run as a job share. Consider small local businesses run by a husband and wife team, the local milkbar, or clothes store or florist shop. Often the husband and wife share the responsibilities of running the business and may work different hours. This working arrangement is highly unlikely to be described as a job share, but that is exactly what it is. Small businesses throughout Australia may actually job share in the form of business partnerships.

■ CAN YOUR ORGANISATION SUPPORT JOB SHARING?

Organisations will find all sorts of reasons to support or decline to support job sharing. At the end of the day it may come down to your ability to understand not only the tangible and intangible elements of the organisation but also the people within it.

Mary remembers talking to one of her brother's friends.

I explained my job share working arrangements to him and he immediately exclaimed that this would not work in his business. His main aim was to serve his customers and he could not see how this could be done effectively unless they could talk to the same person each day of the week. I talked through the following points with him:

- *his business was very vulnerable if that person became ill, left the organisation or was suddenly unavailable for a period of time*
- *continuity in terms of his customers was important; however, did this mean that the customer needed to be called back immediately? If so, was it appropriate that this be done by someone physically located in the workplace? Would it have inconvenienced the customer to get a call back in a couple of days? Was getting the same person to call back the customer immediately the only possible way this could be handled?*
- *if it is so important to get the same staff member to call back the same customer as soon as possible, does this person have to be available eight hours a day, five days a week? Or are there peak times when it is more important to offer this service?*

My brother's friend was not enamoured by any of our discussion. There was no way he could be convinced that any sort of flexible arrangements would work for his business. So we agreed to disagree.

If you find yourself faced with any type of resistance you may need to think of a way through it. A role playing activity (Activity 2) in Chapter 6 will help you with this task.

Not all organisations will find these solutions useful. The management of each organisation has the right to determine which work practices suit their organisation the best. After all it's their money on the line! Almost no organisation could run if all its staff were engaged in job-sharing arrangements. The point is that full timers need flexible workers as much as flexible workers need full timers.

WHAT ABOUT YOUR COLLEAGUES?

The support of co-workers in working flexible hours is crucial. Being flexible around early starts or late finishes is part of working around each other's availability. For instance, this may mean being flexible with your start, finish, meeting and break times on the days you work to accommodate someone else's commitments. Shifting an existing meeting in your diary to help someone who is working full time, but who is already committed at that time, is part of the give and take of the workplace. It also means that others are not having to continually adjust their timetable to suit you, and shows that you can be flexible in order to support others.

We have encountered circumstances where peers have been both supportive and competitive. If peers wish to be competitive and use every opportunity they have to show how much better they are than you — or simply do not want to work in a collaborative manner — then flexible hours can certainly leave you vulnerable. This is where the power issue comes in. The smart thing to do is to pick the forums, events and meetings that are crucial to your job and try to be there. However, at the end of the day the workplace needs relationships to work effectively — these relationships can be developed if both the full-time and flexible-hours workers make the time to do so.

We are both indebted — and always will be — to many in our workplaces who have, through their attitude and approach, facilitated the success of our flexible work arrangements.

WHAT ABOUT YOUR SUPERVISOR?

In many workplaces it is the relationships with co-workers that make the job happen successfully or otherwise. In the cut and thrust of getting the job done one relationship we have found particularly important in terms of working flexibly is that with our immediate supervisor. The person to whom you are directly responsible can often have the most significant effect on negotiating and maintaining flexible work choices regardless of the organisation's stated policies. Along with the organisational culture, the right boss can also make or break a part-time or job-sharing arrangement. Managers bring with them their own individual ideas about people and work management, and they work with these ideas within the organisational context.

Working flexibly requires more discipline in terms of managing your supervisor than may be required when seeking to work in a 'normal' or 'standard' way. It also means gaining and keeping your supervisor's confidence — even when you are not physically present in the workplace, or when someone else is 'being you' in the workplace (as in a job share). In job sharing there is the added challenge of maintaining your supervisor's confidence in you AND your partner. We talk more about this in later chapters.

SUPERVISING EMPLOYEES WHO SHARE A JOB

For flexible working arrangements to succeed the arrangement must be what the organisation wants, and is prepared to support. The direct supervisor (boss) is critical to both of these. It is the direct supervisor who helps determine whether a job can be done in a flexible way and by their very attitude and approach is very influential in the success of the arrangement.

We have come across supervisors who accept flexible work simply as part of the evolution of work. We have also found supervisors who think that the only way to work is to follow in their footsteps — and if that means 40-hour weeks, then tough luck. Job sharing is possible under both regimes — but obviously has a greater chance of success under the former. If you are a supervisor considering managing a job-share arrangement you should first consider the following:

- Are you clear about the requirements of the position proposed as a job share?
- Do you think the job share will mean extra work for you as a supervisor? How do you feel about this?
- Is the type of work in your workplace amenable to a job–share arrangement? Is it possible to share the work across two people? Try to think of examples of where it would work, or where it would not work.
- Have you ever worked with others who worked flexibly? What were your impressions of this arrangement? Does this experience flavour your feelings about flexible working arrangements?
- Looking to the future, how would you know if a job–share arrangement had been successful? Or unsuccessful?
- At the end of the day, do you feel the benefits of a job share will outweigh the benefits of having a single person undertake the job?
- Are you prepared to give it a go?
- Will your attitude help or hinder the arrangement?

CASE STUDY

One of the more visionary CEOs for whom we've worked had an employment philosophy we believe reflected the principle of value creation. She believed in selecting and employing people primarily on the basis of what they might bring to the organisation as individuals. She would create the jobs around them. She felt that this gave her the flexibility to best meet the needs of the organisation at any particular point in time. She was able to skilfully manage the outcomes by employing the right people with the appropriate skills rather than filling specific jobs. It's a subtle difference but it is critical to moving management thinking into a different paradigm for flexible workers.

To provide an insight into how job sharing works from a manager's point of view, we discussed flexible work arrangements with this CEO. She has held a wide variety of CEO positions in both commercial and government enterprises. This appraisal highlights a number of key issues about the requirements of organisations, leaders and employees to make effective use of flexible work practices. (Her words are in italics.)

Having experienced the results of employing a job-share team, what were the advantages and disadvantages?

The organisation has clearly got more than a full-time job equivalent. There is no doubt about that. To get the best for the organisation, you need to accept and acknowledge that people have other elements to their lives that they need to balance. Failing to understand this creates tension, which can only be counter-productive.

Notice the acceptance of the need for work–life balance and the acknowledgment that unhappy employees can work against organisational goals.

I don't believe, however, that it's about entitlement to flexible working hours. I can't accept this. It's about the need for flexibility and balance. You need to have a relationship in which you feel confident in the manner in which the individual is using the flexible arrangements whilst actually providing the contribution to the organisation. Knowing that the arrangements benefit both parties. Recognising that we as individuals are part of a broader community.

This is a clear statement that the benefits of flexible work arrangements must flow both ways — to the organisation and the individual. It is not just about a simple entitlement that employees may have to flexible hours.

The complementarity of contribution has been quite valuable. The relationship between both of you was seamless from where I was sitting. I felt more an observer and a beneficiary of the relationship rather than as an employer.

What the CEO is saying here is that, as manager, she did not have to work harder to make job sharing more effective; in fact, it managed itself and returned benefits to the organisation. This indicates how important it is as job-sharing partners to manage any differences in opinion and style within the job itself and not to look to others, such as managers, to solve things. We often disagreed on how to approach things, but we worked hard on coming up with an agreed approach before we started a task and before we talked to anyone else about it.

The negatives were about not being able to talk to the person that I wanted to talk to. I recognise that this situation can apply regardless of the nature of the working relationship. I sometimes can't get to people who are here full time either. It is also about learning to work with flexible relationships in an organisation. I'm more conscious of this now than earlier — it becomes part of the organisational fabric. It's about the maturity of the organisation to accept flexibility.

Notice here that the CEO equates the difficulty in talking to the person she wants to with someone working full-time hours. It is not the job sharing in itself that caused this problem. Some managers would simply blame the job sharing and say it was not working. Notice also how the job-sharing arrangement has contributed to increasing the CEO's awareness of working with flexible arrangements. Having job sharing in the workplace can be a vehicle for change in itself.

> I feel that you need to be careful not to create dependent relationships. The essence of a good manager is the ability to create an environment of independence. The maturity of subordinates has a lot to do with it. There are ways to organise working lives to build independence.

How did you feel about acquiring a team package through a job-sharing arrangement?

> It was irrelevant to the decision that you were job sharing. The package deal was not part of the attraction. I come from a position that you create work around individuals — that gives you the best flexibility to deliver what you are hoping to deliver. I've got to have a particular person because of what they might bring and what the needs of the organisation are at that time.
>
> I bought two individuals. You just happened to be the package. It's very much about the value that the individual can bring to the organisation. I had a good sense around your personal commitments to the organisation and to roles and jobs.

This may be worth keeping in mind when presenting a job-sharing proposal. One way to position job sharing is as two individuals who want to work in this way — another is as a package. Where you put the emphasis may depend on the organisational needs.

Is there a point at which it becomes non-viable?

> In a larger, ongoing operational management role with significant numbers of staff where your primary job is about leadership, it would not work even in a job-share arrangement. It creates ambiguity.

This is a clear message about this CEO's opinion on the type of job that may not be suited to job sharing.

> It could possibly work with one individual working part time depending on the number of part-time hours, e.g. a four-day-week arrangement. The individual would need to be exceptionally well organised to manage it. I believe that this is a key factor of

any part-time or job-sharing arrangement. As a manager, I would need the same confidence in the arrangement that an individual would require in their job-sharing partner: Have I got an agreement? Have I got a meeting of the minds? Am I sure that the organisation is not going to suffer?

Here the CEO is giving clear ideas about what would convince her to accept a job-sharing arrangement. It may be worth reflecting here on what you know would convince your CEO or manager in your circumstance.

The decision is based on\the characteristics of the individual and the ability to demonstrate confidence that the organisation would not suffer. The leader needs to have an open mind to the opportunities that flexible arrangements offer.

This is a clear statement about the responsibilities of leaders to have an open mind in relation to flexible working arrangements. In our experience not all the people we have worked for have seen this as a leadership responsibility. What do you think is the circumstance in your organisation?

However, I believe that by choosing part time you could be limiting your career potential. A key platform to advance your career must be large-scale management which can't be done in a part-time capacity.

One legal firm we heard about tries to look at flexible hours as a natural part of the career path rather than an obstacle. Perhaps the crucial point here is how much of the career is worked as a flexible arrangement.

WERE SOME ORGANISATIONS MORE OPEN TO FLEXIBLE WORK PRACTICES THAN OTHERS?

I believe that it is the individual manager's perspective rather than the organisational environment that is open to flexibility. Individuals that are open recognise the value of diversity and create the environment that nurtures flexibility. I also believe that organisations in crisis probably need this even more so than those that are highly successful. When you sometimes see organisations in crisis rejecting flexibility and diversity, this can sometimes be a reflection of the individual being narrow rather than the organisation. They are focused on the bottom line rather than looking for opportunities that may be presented by a particular crisis.

Interestingly, this CEO believes that the real time to be flexible is when the organisation is under bottom line pressure. This flies in the face of conventional wisdom that flexible work practices which attract and retain staff are thrown out in times of economic downturn and that job sharing is a luxury.

■ SUMMARY

The nature of your organisation will determine if job sharing is possible. Any organisation is made up of many elements — tangible and intangible, flexibility or inflexibility, public or private. All these elements impact on any job in the organisation. While not every organisation is a candidate for flexible working arrangements, many such arrangements (such as job sharing) can and do work across a number of organisations.

With commitment, consideration and leadership from all parties concerned, flexible arrangements can benefit the organisation and the individual.

chapter 3

Know yourself

- Are you suited to share your job?

- What drives you?

- Developing the right attitude

In this chapter we talk about how knowing yourself can help you see whether you are suited to job sharing. However, just before we leap in to this, we wanted to challenge you to think about whether you have what it takes to succeed as a partner in a job-sharing arrangement. Knowing yourself is all well and good on the one hand, but it is whether you are prepared to apply yourself that makes for success on the other.

Do you have what it takes?

We have spent some time thinking about what type of people job sharing works for and what types of people it doesn't. From our experience it is a mix between wanting the flexibility job sharing offers and being prepared to work hard to make sure that flexibility complements the needs of the workplace. Essentially, you have what it takes to be successful in a job share if you:

- have worked through your life priorities and can clearly place your work ambitions and rewards within those
- can push yourself out of your comfort zone and are prepared to try something new and different — in our opinion, job sharing is not for the faint-hearted but for those who are prepared to challenge the status quo
- can deliver the outcomes for the job in the time available
- are able to work collaboratively with your job-sharing partner, which means sharing control and trusting your partner with the positioning of your career
- can meet your needs in the workplace in less hours than the traditional worker (we all work for different reasons — can you get what you want in less hours than the traditional worker?)
- have the drive and energy required to keep trying and experimenting to find out what works the best for the two of you and your organisation.

After reading this, do you think you have what it takes?

■ ARE YOU SUITED TO SHARE YOUR JOB?

While many of us ponder the reasons why we might want to share our job with someone, most of us do not take the extra step to consider *how* to make this happen. It often seems far too difficult to seriously contemplate. The idea may be in lots of heads, but few people talk about the strategies needed to transform the idea into reality.

The many issues and strategies that need to be thought and worked through to make part-time work and job sharing a success can sometimes be overwhelming. They do, in fact, fall into two broad categories that balance into a neat equation.

$$\text{Job-sharing success} = \frac{\text{Knowing what to do (the practicalities)} \times \text{Strategies for sustainability}}{\text{Self-knowing (understandings)}}$$

Most of our research shows that the *Practicalities* is where most people focus when thinking about how they might create greater flexibility in their lives. They think about how to:

- cover workload over a certain number of reduced hours
- ensure that quality of outcome does not suffer
- approach their boss for agreements
- find an organisation that is family friendly and therefore more amenable to flexible work routines
- find or get on with a job–share partner.

These are all very important elements, but for those who seek to build a career and maintain flexibility over a long period of time, these practicalities need to be underpinned by a set of deeper *Understandings*. This chapter focuses on these understandings.

Having a good understanding of your values, goals and ambitions helps maintain focus when trying to balance and prioritise work and personal activities. Being aware of your strengths and weaknesses, how you feel about fundamental issues in your life and what sorts of things keep you going through tough times becomes even more important in a part-time or job-sharing situation.

Developing these understandings is a useful life skill in general; however, in a part-time job-sharing environment it becomes an important part of the formula for long-term success. These understandings provide support in an environment which becomes magnified from both your own perspective and those around you. This magnification is often brought about by virtue of just being different in a culture that is centred around a full-time career. It is brought about by the intensity created by performing and delivering in timeframes which are in reality shorter than those for full-time colleagues. The bottom line is, you can manage with only a scant level of these understandings, but to thrive you need a deeper level to underpin the decisions you make on the day-to-day practicalities of establishing and living in a job-sharing situation.

■ WHAT DRIVES YOU?

Taking some time to gain a better understanding of yourself may help you to keep focused when the inevitable conflicts arise while trying to manage flexible work options. To understand yourself you need to know what factors drive you, how you respond under pressure, and what are your strengths and weaknesses.

In the past we have used some tried and true tools and techniques which we will describe briefly and which you may find useful to help you gain a better insight into yourself. We have found that even just one or two of them has helped us understand ourselves and each other better, and therefore helped us appreciate how we may respond in our flexible arrangement. This is not intended to be an exhaustive list, but it does provide you with some ideas to start you off on your understanding quest.

A LIFE MISSION

Have you ever asked yourself, 'Where am I heading in my life and what do I want to achieve?' Stephen Covey in *The 7 Habits of Highly Effective People* (1989) writes about 'beginning with the end in mind' and gives an outline of how to write a life mission statement. Going through the mission writing process can provide a sense of direction and priority in life. A mission statement can be a useful grounding tool when the challenges of life — let alone the challenge of working part time — become a little overwhelming. It can also help if you return to your mission statement often and reflect upon what you are trying to achieve and what you value. Later in the chapter, Mary shares her mission statement with you.

> **The mission statement is essentially a reference point. It helps to return to a reference point to remind yourself from time to time what's important.**

Your mission statement (or reference point) does not have to be written on a piece of paper — it can be a regular, relaxing or meditative activity, a special place, or even a piece of prose or music — as long as it acts as a powerful and unambiguous reminder of what you are trying to achieve and what you value above all else.

If you are unable to find an activity which helps you prioritise and direct your life, you may find job sharing challenging. Working in an environment where most people are undertaking the traditional 9 a.m. to 5 p.m. hours while you are not only job sharing but trying to integrate outside commitments as well creates conflicting priorities. As we have said, clear priorities can really help — otherwise you may well be looking at a pressure cooker for disaster.

ASPECTS OF SELF

Think about what motivates you. Some hint of this could be in your mission statement, but essentially motivators and mission statements are different. The first is an outline of where you want to focus in the long term and the latter what you will respond to in attempting to achieve this. There are many psychological theories which focus on human needs and how they drive our behaviours or motivate us to action. We suggest you take some time to understand what fundamental needs or drivers you have which may affect the way you respond in given situations you might encounter in the workplace. As they say, forewarned is forearmed.

We were fortunate to have undertaken a leadership development program a few years ago. At this stage we had already been job sharing for over four years. Part of this program introduced us to the motivation work by David McClelland. To paraphrase what was discussed in the program, there are three main motivators:

- the need to achieve
- the need to affiliate
- the need for power.

Further, our motive profile is developed in our late teens and early twenties. He uses responses to a series of pictures to determine the motive profile. People usually receive a rating across all three motivators. We have developed a worksheet, 'Understanding yourself' (Chapter 6, Activity 3), to provide you with some hints to help you know yourself better. Our personal comments later in this chapter will also provide you with some of our personal learnings from this work.

It is possible that one particular motive profile is better suited to job sharing than others. It is also interesting to think about whether job sharing could work if both partners had an equally high need for power, affiliation or achievement. This could be challenging if both wanted to control a project, for example, or both wanted to be acknowledged for their achievement when one had contributed more than the other.

> We think the important thing for job-sharing partners is to be aware of each other's motive profile and think about how to make them complementary.

You will see later in this chapter how we worked our personal motive profiles so that they complemented each other. If you are both high achievers it may be worth thinking about the best way to acknowledge and support each other in this — and it may be worth having a strategy for when one member is acknowledged for work undertaken by the other. Success is about expending the effort to have the knowledge about the other person, and then using that knowledge to make the job sharing happen successfully.

PERSONAL STYLE

Have you ever thought about your personal style? How would your style fit with the style of your boss, your peers and your subordinates? How does it reflect your preferred mode of operation? An understanding of personal style has helped us understand why we sometimes get on each other's nerves and, conversely, why we just seem to be able to fuse in some magical way.

There are probably as many tools available to provide these insights as there are consultants offering personal development courses. They all provide useful insights at different levels. Some of these include The Team Management Index (TMI) developed by Margersion and McCann, The Myers–Briggs Type Indicator (MBTI) and the Geier's DiSC Profile. We have used all these tools at different times to provide us with insights into our personalities and how they are reflected in our behaviours or style at work. There are of course others, equally as reputable, which we have not had experience with to date.

We found the Team Management Index useful not only because it gave us personal insights but it also helped us better understand some of the dynamics of working as a job-sharing team. The TMI applies Carl Jung's philosophies on personality types to a team situation and measures how people in the work situation:

- prefer to relate with others
- gather and use information
- make decisions
- organise themselves and others.

Our TMI results below show our role preferences.

	MAJOR ROLE PREFERENCE	RELATED PREFERENCE
Angela	Creator–Innovator	Thruster–Organiser
Mary	Explorer–Promoter	Thruster–Organiser

To quickly summarise what this means:

Creator–Innovators:
- generate ideas
- are independent and wish to experiment
- may contradict existing systems and methods.

Explorer–Promoters:
- take up ideas and get people enthusiastic
- identify and use information and resources
- are not always good at controlling detail.

Thruster–Organisers:
- like getting things done
- turn ideas into reality
- can be impatient about getting things done.

This very brief summary shows some of the elements which in combination produced a powerful job-sharing partnership. We had complementary modes of preference which were underpinned by the same drive to get to an outcome. We became a force for change and adaptation. However, the high achievement drive in both of us did, on occasions, lead us to taking on more work than could be achieved. When working part time this needs to be carefully managed.

It will be helpful for you to reflect upon your personal style and we have developed some points for your reflection. Turn to Activity 3, 'Your personal style'.

We both had some interesting feedback at one stage which suggested that we did not spend sufficient time coaching and developing our staff. People with our TMI profiles coupled with a high-achievement orientation can sometimes appear highly tasked focused with little time for developing and coaching staff. From our perspectives, it felt that we were spending adequate time with staff, but we struggled to work out why they might take so long to work things out! So knowing how we prefer to operate in a team helps to draw on our individual as well as collective strengths and weaknesses. In addition, knowing how our staff prefer to operate also helps us understand them better.

As we mentioned earlier, another useful tool is Geier's DiSC Profile which identifies, measures and assists in benchmarking both individual work personalities and work organisational profiles. It provides a number of key pointers and characteristics of personal and work style preferences. This is important when you're operating on limited hours. It is also vital in building and maintaining strong relationships with job-sharing partners.

> **Understanding your own unique behavioural pattern or style and being able to quickly deduce that of the people you interact with in the workplace helps maximise the productivity or effectiveness of your interactions.**

Another important insight that we have had over the years in using these tools is that our results have changed over time and with the different roles that we have taken on. This highlights that they are only guides and not to be taken as gospel. Nor are they intended to be consulted like astrological guides. It is also important to remember that, as we undergo new experiences and grow as individuals, our style, behaviours, attitudes and the impact that they have on others will also evolve. It is therefore important that we continue through life (in flexible work conditions or otherwise) to take time out to gain a better sense of ourself.

Again we have considered whether a particular TMI or DiSC profile is better suited to job sharing than another. We do not believe so. However, because two of you are presenting in the workplace to do one job, knowledge of personal styles and preferences is crucial. As we mention later — whether we like it or not — comparisons will happen when job sharing. So if your personal styles or preferences are similar, your lack of variation may become a point of comment (for instance, 'Angela and Mary are just so alike — they think identically, it is no use trying to change their minds'). Alternatively, if they are different they may become polarised ('Angela and Mary are like chalk and cheese, it is so confusing working with them').

Be mindful of such comparisons of your personal styles and preferences. Our experience is that it can leave you typecast as individuals and as job-sharing partners. Our suggestion would be to work on operating in your non-preferred style occasionally so that the organisation gets to see the whole personalities of both of you.

■ DEVELOPING THE RIGHT ATTITUDE

Here we share our personal experiences of what motivated us to job share and how we worked with our drivers — our personal styles and preferences. You will see that we are very different people and worked hard at making our job sharing happen successfully.

MOTIVATING MARY

My personal mission statement reflects the number of priorities I have in my life. I think about it regularly and make changes as I think appropriate. At this point in my life working part time is one of the ways I live out my mission. I've included part of my mission statement below.

MARY'S MISSION STATEMENT
- *To break the pattern — for myself, for women in general, for working women seeking balance, and for all those who seek to move beyond where they are currently.*
- *To value excellence and the pursuit of it — to seek to make my life the difference between good and very good (or excellent). To not be satisfied with second best.*
- *To grasp the moment. To live more fully NOW. To embrace life with passion and commitment. To risk.*
- *To be relaxed and yet fulfil my promise. To discern the need for active time and for quiet time. To be balanced.*

I find that working flexible hours means my motive profile in effect becomes condensed. By my own analysis, I have a high need for achievement, a medium to low need for affiliation and a medium need for power. This means that at work — where I choose to limit my time — I have to work very hard at maintaining relationships because at the end of the day I value achievement over socialising. In the past, feedback from my staff confirmed this as they have made it clear that I don't spend enough time with them! Accordingly, I now prioritise meetings with my staff.

As for my need for power, this gets squeezed into my flexible hours. One of the big things I have learnt about working flexible hours is the art of letting go of the control of the total project. To a large extent this means having enough 'control' over my job to do it effectively but not as much 'control' as others in the workplace. (There are some real advantages to this as it prepares you for a management role where time is always tight). By choosing not to be in the workplace as often as anyone else is I have to rely on others — and this means letting go sometimes (but only to those I trust!).

One of the interesting side effects of my high need for achievement is that I respond to external feedback that is both frequent and specific. This is another issue for those working flexible hours. You need to squeeze in appointments all day long, usually to talk about what we will try to achieve next, which doesn't allow much time for others to give me feedback — yet I crave it.

So you can see that understanding what my motivators are helps keep me on an even keel in the workplace. This hasn't fallen into place overnight, but it allows me to manage myself and keep things in perspective when I am unsure of what is happening to me in the workplace.

MOTIVATING ANGELA

As outlined earlier in this chapter, I have encountered a number of tools over the years which I have used to varying degrees which have helped me gain a deeper self-knowledge. The tools described are by no means exhaustive. Another point that I'd like to make is that they are very formal approaches to exploring a sense of self. There are many other tools, formal and informal, that can help you develop a deeper sense of self-awareness.

First, a little more on the formal. A key learning for me early on in my career was gained through the Myers–Briggs Type Indicator (MBTI). My MBTI profile is ITP — Introverted, Intuitive, Thinking, Perceiving. I realised at the time that this confirmed, or rather reflected, the mode in which I felt most comfortable. That is, I tend to be by nature an analytical and introspective person. This means that I can also be very self-critical. I believe that this has proven to be both a strength as well as a weakness for me. Over the years I have intuitively combined this knowledge with a number of informal tools to develop a strong sense of what is important to me, a clear set of personal values and what I hope to achieve. As seen from Mary's personal comments, these are key elements in developing a mission statement. I believe that I also have a good sense of where I need development (this is usually when I'm out of my comfort zone) and what I'm good at.

Some of the informal tools that I have used are probably better described as behaviours. The key ones have included:

- The ability to undertake objective self-analysis. *This has helped me to identify my strengths and weaknesses. This is important knowledge for anyone who always strives to do better, but particularly so in a job-sharing partnership, which is essentially a team approach. Knowing each other's strengths and weaknesses opens up a clearer path to developing complementary skills as well as compensating for each other should it be necessary. In the end, it means a higher quality of service is delivered.*
- To religiously identify lessons learnt from key work and personal successes and failures. *Rather than being an introspective activity, I have found that this is best talked through with trusted colleagues and mentors. Identifying lessons for me has always led to a stronger focus on outcome and cleared the path to new and exciting opportunities.*
- Having a personal grounding point. *This could be a person, place or thing that brings you back to the focus of what is absolutely fundamental in your life. A strong grounding point has been invaluable in helping me sort through work and personal priorities to achieve a better balance in my life. My grounding point has always been outside of work, and I guess that is why I may find it possibly a little easier than others to remember to keep work in a balanced perspective.*

As for my motive profile, like Mary I believe that I have a strong need for achievement. Another key ingredient to a powerful job-sharing partnership. However, I feel that I also have a strong need for affiliation. A successful job-sharing arrangement has provided me with a great deal of satisfaction in this area. I believe that my need for affiliation has fuelled the energy that I have invested in maintaining partnership and team arrangements.

Appreciating that not everyone will have access to the various tests that can lead to understanding motivators, we have included a worksheet in Chapter 6, Activity 4 that may provide some insight on the spot. This may give insight into those areas of work life that provide job satisfaction, frustration and stress. By reflecting on these you may get an idea of some of your work motivations.

■ SUMMARY

From our experience, we believe it is important to prepare yourself and understand the role of personality when taking up a flexible working arrangement such as job sharing. This puts you in good store for a successful partnership. We end this chapter with reference to Activity 5 in Chapter 6. This challenges you to think about whether flexible working arrangements are for you.

chapter 4

Implementing job sharing

- Finding the opportunity

- Finding a job-sharing partner

- Positioning yourself in the organisation

- Rewards for flexible workers

- Fitting the needs of the organisation

- Choosing your work partner

- The job-sharing proposal

- Avenues for future change

At one stage, we were in the middle of a downsize. Our employer had reconsidered its policy and we had a job for another three months — maximum. We started working our networks and decided that, while we would prefer to remain in a job share, the real issue was remaining in employment. If we needed to split, we would. We had put together separate résumés and were making a list of our joint achievements when our boss came over to us. He told us he'd been talking to a number of people to see if anyone was interested in taking us both on in a job share, and they'd been saying, 'We can't afford the luxury of a job share'. We looked at each other and laughed — job sharing certainly didn't feel like a luxury to us, it felt like damn hard work!

What we have set out to do in this chapter is to help you with all the issues that need to be sorted out before you start a job-sharing arrangement. Chapters 2 and 3 have covered some of the preparatory work: Are you suited to job sharing? Is it viable within your organisation?, etc. Chapter 4 is really all about what needs to be done to put it into practice. We have tried to cover the whole range of things to consider — but don't panic if you haven't got them all squared off before you start. Just try to cover them all over time. Good luck!

Just another note before you start. You will find that we refer to working 'flexibly' in this chapter and Chapter 5. Take this to mean as working other than the 'typical' hours (both in terms of length and timing) a full-time worker in your industry would work. We also refer to 'part-time hours' — this is because as an individual in a job share you are likely to be working part time, while the job is shared across full-time hours — as individuals you are likely to be working less than full time.

■ FINDING THE OPPORTUNITY

Finding the opportunity to work flexibly is not always easy, making the opportunity is another thing altogether.

Sometimes the job you are in or are thinking of going into is already established as a flexible hours/job-sharing arrangement. Such positions are advertised in the local and national papers from time to time. However, our experience is that more often than not, and particularly at a senior level, the job is established as a full-time standard hours position. In fact, it may never have been envisioned as anything other than this — so here is where the challenge begins. Issues you may need to consider include whether:
• the work can be undertaken on a flexible hours basis
• you have the expertise to undertake the job on reduced hours
• you have some flexibility around the times you are planning not to be in the workplace
• a drop in income is involved.

Let's look at these one at a time.

Can the work be undertaken on a flexible hours basis?

Another way of putting this is: can the organisation still achieve its goals and have you work flexible hours? Obviously this depends, at least partly, on the type of work involved. Where a full-time presence is necessary across standard hours it may simply not be realistic to have the job undertaken on a flexible hours basis. However, the mind-set that may need challenging is whether you need to be there full time and across standard hours. Our experience is that working flexibly certainly hones the mind in terms of the essential work! It just comes down to convincing others in the workplace that the quality of work will not suffer if a flexible arrangement is trialled. However, there is no question that some customer service or similar positions may require full-time responsiveness. If this requires full-time *presence* as opposed to *availability* then the flexible hours option may simply not be realistic. In this situation you may be able to consider the possibilities of a job-sharing arrangement.

Do you have the expertise to undertake the job flexibly?

You will need to have the competence (let alone the confidence!!) to take on the job as if you are present full time, working standard hours. For instance, if a meeting or event occurred at a time when you were not there, in order to do your job effectively you may need to assume knowledge (or actually have found out what happened) as if you were there. Obviously all full-time workers do this occasionally when they are double booked.

We have worked flexibly — both part time and job sharing at a senior level — so it can be done! We've sometimes found it easier to 'assume' knowledge, particularly after some time in the organisation when the learning curve is not so steep. One way of gaining the expertise necessary is to (if possible) undertake the job on a full-time basis for a period of time (e.g. six weeks, three months), then work flexibly. If your organisation agrees, this can be very useful in setting up the foundation for a flexible arrangement — whether part time or job sharing. Taking on a new job under flexible arrangements, in a new work area, or in an organisation that you haven't worked in before, can be very stressful.

Do you have some flexibility around the times you are planning not to be in the workplace?

Having some flexibility around the times we planned not to be present in the workplace certainly helped a lot. We are both aware that the world of work will go on without us and in some cases it was simply inevitable that one of us would be needed in the workplace on a day we had planned to be elsewhere. Such circumstances happened occasionally for a variety of reasons. For instance, it was the only time we could get a certain group of people together or one of us had a context or history with a project that simply could not be transferred to the other. On these occasions we simply re-scheduled our time and came in. Provided this did not happen on a regular basis we felt the benefits far outweighed the disadvantages.

A drop in income is involved

It is all very well to talk about working flexibly, but if the reality means a reduction in income, it is important this is sorted out early in the journey. Many people work the hours they work because they cannot afford otherwise. Mary recalls:

> When my husband and I embarked on the flexible working hours journey we sat down and carefully planned our budget to see what was possible. We recognised that we needed to carefully anticipate our expenses for the year before taking a step to reduce our income. At this stage we were early into our mortgage. With careful planning we gave it a go and managed it from there.

■ FINDING A JOB-SHARING PARTNER

If you are starting to consider whether a job-sharing arrangement could work, the next challenge then becomes finding an actual partner. Later in the chapter we talk about some of the personal and professional qualities you might look for in a prospective job-sharing partner. It is clear, however, that the hardest part is actually finding a 'prospective field' of potential partners.

In recognition of the ever-increasing demand for flexibility, many human resources areas are creating reference lists of people seeking part-time or job-sharing arrangements. Such a list was not conceived of at the time we started job sharing. One of the important lessons we've learnt is that to find a work partner, it is important to continually cultivate and explore your network of friends, colleagues and peers. This is where you may often find people who share similar ideas and desires about work and life balance.

Here are some novel ways to seek a job-sharing partner:
- Consider other people in your current work situation — do you think there is anyone who is looking for some flexibility in their work and who you would consider as a job-sharing partner?
- Attend an appropriate conference (e.g. work–life balance workshops) and network the participants.
- If you are aware of a job that is about to be advertised, ask if the job could be considered (i.e. advertised) as a job share and talk to others about applying with you.
- Advertise in your work area and local newspaper for a job-sharing partner.
- Seek a recruitment agency that matches flexible workers with flexible employers.

- Look for opportunities in your personal life (e.g. where other working parents meet and chat).
- Seek help from your mentor.
- Talk to academic experts in the field.
- Search the net for how others did it.

In hindsight we actually did a lot of learning about how to set-up a job-sharing arrangement and how to then operate within that structure 'on the job'. So things like how we would split our hours and how we would share the work we learnt by trial and error (and sometimes error and error!). You do not have to do it this way. In the pages ahead we ask you to consider the best type of job share for you and your organisation — hopefully before you start in job sharing. This will allow you to 'hit the ground running' and not have to manage sorting out the mechanics of job sharing while learning a brand new job, for at least one of you. In this next section we discuss the professional and personal attributes we consider useful in a successful job share.

■ POSITIONING YOURSELF IN THE ORGANISATION

Having a good knowledge of your organisation's psyche allows you to maximise your positioning within the organisation. It will allow you to see where you can match your strengths to the organisation, and how you can maximise the opportunities presented by working flexibly. The following are some ideas on how we have done this in the past.

First a short story from Angela that illustrates simply the inappropriate assumptions that people can make.

In my early part-time days I was once asked whether I was going to continue with the arrangement. When I replied that I would for as long as I could, I was asked, 'When are you going to get serious?'

This throwaway line by a colleague alerted me to the fact that people who work in a part-time or job-sharing arrangement can be viewed differently in the workplace simply because they do not operate within the organisational norm. This meant that not only did I need to position myself as an individual in the organisation, but also as a part-time and job-sharing individual. I felt that I needed to almost educate those around me about what being a part-timer meant in the work context. It certainly did not mean that I was looking for an easy ride!

We have focused on three key elements in positioning yourself in the workplace — commitment, flexibility and clear priorities.

COMMITMENT

It is important to not only be committed but also to actively show your commitment to the goals of the organisation. As the jibe from our colleagues in Angela's story suggests, those in flexible working arrangements can be seen to have a lesser commitment to the workplace than those who work full time. We believe success in a flexible arrangement cannot be achieved with anything other than a very high level of commitment. In reality, commitment is not a quantity measure. More so, it is a reflection of your priorities and how strongly you feel about them. Commitment is demonstrated in your behaviour, attitude and the energy you are willing to invest. This is a critical point of leverage for success in flexible work and, particularly, job-sharing approaches.

The importance you place on achieving your personal and organisational work outcomes is a reflection of your commitment.

FLEXIBILITY

This may seem to be stating the obvious, that is, if you work within a flexible arrangement, that it must follow you are being flexible. This is not necessarily the case. Working in a narrower time frame from those around you can sometimes create a perception of inflexibility. For example, not being available for meetings on the days you don't normally work. It is important to create back-up strategies to ensure your availability does not impede the normal workings of the organisation. We found that in supportive organisations this usually works both ways. When you demonstrate you are prepared to be flexible then the organisation is also more mindful and considerate of your working needs. Here are some practical tips on how to enhance your flexibility.

- Rescheduling care arrangements for children or other dependents including short-term and alternative care, and alternative transport arrangements should you be delayed or need to go into the office unexpectedly. This may mean organising alternative carseats/wheelchairs for transport, having packed lunches, snacks etc. on standby, as well as a packed change of clothes.
- Consider transport practicalities such as does the car have petrol, money for parking meters, etc., change to purchase train/tram tickets, etc., and what is the latest time you can leave the workplace (and have you made this clear to others) in order to meet your commitments outside work.
- You will also need to think about your own self-care practicalities:
  - what do you need to reschedule (hairdresser, dentist etc.)?
  - do you have clean clothes to wear?
  - do other members of the family have clean clothes for the next day?
  - what arrangements are there for dinner?
  - do you have a record of date and time worked?

- what are your back-up arrangements if someone you care for is ill on this day?
- what are your back-up arrangements if an unplanned event occurs (e.g. keys locked in the car, train timetable changed etc.)?
- are you expecting to have extra time worked recognised, acknowledged, stored as time in lieu and have you made this clear?
- how will you take care of yourself after you have worked the extra hours?
- what do you consider to be a reasonable number of times per month that you are asked to be flexible?
- will you expect to be reimbursed for this extra time?

CLEAR PRIORITIES

Having both work and personal priorities clearly outlined in your own mind as well as for your work colleagues immediately positions you within the organisation. Naturally, the priorities that you choose and how you balance work and personal issues become your demonstration of your commitment and flexibility.

Activity 6 will help you to consider these three key elements in your personal solution.

■ REWARDS FOR FLEXIBLE WORKERS

As mentioned previously, working in a job share means you are moving out of the main-stream work environment. This means it may be worthwhile to consider how the dollars you earn are calculated in terms of the financial return you receive. The traditional way of calculating this may not simply translate full-time arrangements into a job-sharing equivalent.

One of the most tangible remuneration criteria remains hours of input. This becomes increasingly so when trying to maintain relativity between two people who are both focused on developing and delivering quality outcomes. Usually reward structures that sit above basic remuneration frameworks go beyond the simple input equations to recognise outcomes and value added. Experience has taught us that is where we needed to put most of our attention when negotiating pay and work conditions.

By asking our employers to focus on the value we could add to the organisation and the subsequent outcomes we agreed to achieve, we were placing ourselves on an equal footing with all other colleagues (part time, full time, casual and contract). The minimum hours worked became the base level (one of the things considered) rather than funda-mental (the only thing considered).

One of the questions that has been occupying our minds is whether it is possible to look at the whole package rather than just a pro-rata equivalent. You may trade a cut in pay for more time in your personal life. The teleworker may trade two hours travelling time each day for working eight hours at home, which suits them much better than ten hours out of the home. Another teleworker may trade their love of the work, which is not available in their local area, for the flexibility of working online interstate and travelling long distances every second week. The judgments here are subjective and need to be sorted out between the worker and the organisation. However, we think it will be the intangible aspects of the organisational psyche that will determine the possibilities of flexible employment.

Knowing how organisations treat rewards and bonuses may also give you a feel for their approach to flexible employment. Does the organisation think rewards, such as bonuses, realistic for flexible workers such as those in a job share? Again this depends on the tangible and intangible aspects of organisational psyche (referred to in Chapter 2). The policies covering this may simply state that such circumstances are to be dealt with on a pro-rata basis. But is pro-rata really the answer? The questions that you could ask yourself are, 'If I am paid for 25 hours a week, but my productivity is obviously higher, does a straight pro-rata really apply?' Or alternatively, 'Does the higher rate of productivity roughly equate to the flexibility I am granted by not being in the workplace the same hours as others are?' 'If I am only coming into the office two days a week (or four a fortnight), but I am on call all weekend, does pro-rata really apply?' These are very big questions and we think they relate to a shift in a paradigm regarding flexible workers.

Activity 7 provides a checklist for your remuneration negotiation with your employer. It would be good to discuss this with your job-sharing partner before you begin negotiations.

■ FITTING THE NEEDS OF THE ORGANISATION

The needs of the organisation that has agreed to your job-sharing or flexible work arrangements will also influence heavily the arrangement that you finally settle upon. The practicalities of how you will get your work done and what expectations the organisation will have of being able to contact you regardless of whether it's your designated day in the office are important things to consider as you step out of the full-time routine.

MANAGING THE WORK

Managing quality in a complex work environment is all about delivering on the job.

The organisations we worked for were quite happy for us to work a six-day week in our job-sharing arrangement. This allowed one of us to work Monday to Wednesday and the other to work from Wednesday to Friday. Wednesday became our hand-over day. We were very aware that as a unit we cost 1.2 times that of someone else at our level. However, the organisations we worked for would agree that, given the work we covered, they certainly got value for money. We certainly felt they got their 'pound of flesh'.

Before embarking on your job-sharing arrangement, consider the most effective way for the job to be split and what will work best for you and your job-sharing partner. This will clarify how you will provide value for money for your organisation. As the <www.ivillage.co.uk> website states, there are three main types of job share:

> Shared responsibility — *there is no division of duties. The job-share partners are interchangeable. This works well for jobs where the work flows continuously. It demands a high level of communication and co-ordination — and that the partners are well matched.*
>
> Divided responsibility — *works well when work can be split into different client groups or different projects. Each partner has their own case-load or project, which they focus on during working hours. If the partners don't know each other well, this can be a suitable way to arrange the job-share.*
>
> Unrelated responsibility — *the partners perform completely separate tasks, while working in the same department. It's rather like two part-time jobs running in tandem and fits situations where the partners have different skills.*[10]

You will need to think carefully about which type of job share you are hoping to enter. The experiences related in this book refer to what was primarily a 'shared responsibility'. Activity 8 explores the three types of job sharing a little further.

In any job, clear outcomes are crucial. The organisations we have worked for have had 'performance agreements' whereby the outcomes and behaviours expected of each individual are spelt out. These are reviewed every three to six months. When job sharing, we always had a joint performance agreement. This meant the assessment of our performance was inextricably linked. We both have high expectations in terms of delivery of outcomes and behaviours so this was not an issue for us. We were also fortunate that the organisations we worked for were happy for us to work this way as well. This is an example of our work goals matching our organisation's values. You may like to think about how you would like your partnership performance to be measured.

So having clarified the outcomes necessary for our job, it was important to work out how to get the job done between the two of us. This is a challenge all job sharers must face. As our work was project based, we tackled this by splitting the projects between us, so each of us could take a lead on various projects. This meant that each project was managed primarily by one of us, with the other supporting these projects on the days the other was not at work. This worked well for the majority of our projects. It meant we had to understand each other's projects to some extent and that a real team approach was necessary. Some of the projects were so big that they required daily management, in which case we shared joint responsibility. However, regardless of the project arrangements, we were both equally accountable for delivery against all project outcomes. This required a lot of communication between us to make sure we 'spoke with one voice' (we discuss this further in the next chapter).

Like many jobs at senior level, just getting the job done can seem to take up all the time in the week. However, we were committed to continuing our professional development while job sharing. You may like to consider if this is a priority for you. Again we were fortunate to be able to be a little bit flexible about the days we worked. (Note this is another example of an organisation supporting our work goals with its values.) This enabled us, where possible, to attend professional development or key events together. Where this was not possible we debriefed the development opportunity with each other so that we both learnt from the experience. You may need to consider how you will manage this between the two of you.

COVERING THE TIME YOU AREN'T THERE (AND MOSTLY EVERYONE ELSE IS!)

This is a big one, particularly in terms of mindset. One of the first things that may occur in someone's (usually your supervisor's) mind is 'but who is going to do the work when you aren't here?' Obviously, if you have a job-share partner you are halfway there. If not, you need to have a ready response. There are a number of options, such as:

- being contactable during the times you are not physically in the workplace, for example, by having a mobile phone or at least an answering machine
- being available to come in on those days if an 'emergency' occurs, having other ways of meeting a key deadline, such as working late at night if necessary
- organising to have emails sent home so that urgent issues can be addressed
- having your work phone forwarded to another number, such as your mobile phone
- arranging voicemail for your work phone with an option for contact if they need a reply with 24 hours
- being clear about how much of your work is *urgent* and needs to be addressed immediately and how much can actually wait until you are in the workplace (If you have historic data, this could be useful, e.g. over the past 15 months there were six deadlines under 24 hours, five under three days and two that needed to be met within a week.)
- asking another part-time worker (who works the times when you don't) to keep an eye on your workplace with you returning the favour when she/he is not there.

Obviously if any of these options interfere too much with your time out of the workplace, they are not real options. However, these options have worked for us and worked well. One of the main issues is that such concepts challenge the traditional mindset of the workplace — 'but if you are not here then who will get the work done?'

REALISTIC EXPECTATIONS

A word about expectations and a touch of reality. We have had to be very careful not to set ourselves up to become superwomen. To avoid striving to be superwomen we have had to identify the essentials and the priorities in our work and outside work life. Some of the questions you might like to ask yourself to help you keep your work priorities manageable and therefore your expectations realistic include:

- Who is it crucial that I see and speak to — superiors, peers, staff member, mentor?
- How much time do I need to spend with each?
- What subject matter do I need to cover with each of them?
- What email do I want to send?
- Which email must I reply to?
- How do I determine this?
- What are my key short-term deliverables for this week?
- What are my key long-term deliverables for this week?
- What are my deadlines for this week?
- How will I manage them?
- What long-term planning do I need to think about?
- What development needs do I need to address?
- What am I avoiding or putting off? (Sometimes asking yourself this question can help you get to the nitty gritty and ask whether you are putting something off because you simply don't want to do it. It can help you get to the nub of what really needs to be done.)
- Have you made enough time for those activities which you like and do well (refer to the Passion Chart — Activity 4)? Remember this is where your job satisfaction will come from. Make sure you allow for this sort of work every week!

These questions are ones that someone working full time may wish to answer as well.

Usually this type of prioritising is done subconsciously or automatically. But when the job feels like it's getting away from you, you will find it is useful to return to the list to help get you back on track. Obviously the list can change from week to week — remember, the key is to really try to peel away the things that are nice to do and the things that have to be done. It can be particularly challenging at the end of your working week when the occasional social function is being organised — you may be forced to ask yourself whether after-work drinks with your colleagues are 'nice to have' or 'must be done'. Sometimes it is both!

■ CHOOSING YOUR WORK PARTNER

Choosing the right partner can be more of an art than a science. Our experience has taught us that it requires knowledge of the practicalities of the job, intuition, insight and, most importantly, serendipity. On the 'science' side there are key things to consider such as whether your potential job-sharing partner has the skills and attributes that will help get the job done. On the 'art' side of things it is the connection, the relationship between the two people involved in the job sharing that really makes things work or not work. Our experiences have provided us with some insights which we hope in sharing with you will make your choice a more fully considered one.

The following short story from Angela shows how it all began.

Mary and I first met in 1990 as participants of a managerial development scheme run by our employer at the time. Our paths crossed again a couple of years later as we both commenced work in the same corporate marketing area. We were both working in demanding marketing and planning positions providing internal consultancy advice to various business lines. Both of us were in our early thirties, relatively newly married and considering having children. We quickly recognised that to continue to expand our careers, have children and build a marriage would be difficult if we continued to work full time. We realised that working part time would provide the flexibility that was needed to better balance the needs of work, family and self.

So the job-sharing notion was born. During numerous lunch-time strolls we fantasised about working in a job-sharing partnership without really having any idea how we might make it a reality.

A year or so later, I was offered an exciting marketing position by a man who I knew was flexible, always open to innovation and was a great role model and leader. At that time, Mary was considering reducing her full-time load to part time following the birth of her first child and I was hoping to reduce my workload to focus more strongly on some personal aspects of my life. As he spoke to me, I felt instantly that the planets had aligned. I proposed to him that I take on the new role in a shared arrangement with Mary (with whom he had worked in the past). He thought it was a great idea and said that as far as he was concerned he was the winner as he was getting 'the value of two for the price of one'.

And so our job-sharing adventure commenced.

We recognise that we were very fortunate in having a potential boss who welcomed the idea of job sharing with open arms. We had both worked with this man at different stages in the past and he had valued our work as individuals. This obviously laid the groundwork for his acceptance. For those of you who don't find yourself in this situation, later in this chapter we discuss the idea of an actual job-sharing proposal.

PROFESSIONAL ATTRIBUTES

Complementary strengths and weaknesses can bring benefits to a job-sharing arrangement. Our experience is that there needs to be a common set of attributes upon which to build the relationship. We think these are:

- appropriate skills and knowledge
- a shared work ethic
- ability to share control
- shared level of commitment to the arrangement.

Appropriate skills and knowledge

Although in a shared arrangement, the roles and responsibilities may be shared, this does not necessarily mean that the skills or knowledge of each partner need to parallel. However, they do need to be adequate to get the job done and done well. Job-sharing partners, like anyone else in the workplace, can learn on the job via training or in a number of ways. A base level of competency is necessary for both members so that the value the arrangement adds to the organisation is immediately apparent.

In fact, we realised only after we'd worked together for some time that our skills actually complemented each other. This provided the employer, our managers and staff an opportunity they would not normally get through an individual. As we learnt to work together, the quality of the decisions we made and the products we delivered increased. We became our own critics, we used each other as soundingboards, and we brought our individual perspectives together, often resulting in more innovative solutions.

A shared work ethic

> A shared work ethic is a characteristic that can sometimes be overlooked or taken for granted until it suddenly becomes an issue.

A shared work ethic or belief about the importance of delivering quality outputs is vital. Where different standards or expectations exist this can become an issue that creates tension and disharmony if one partner begins to feel they are carrying the larger share of the partnership on their shoulders. During our job-sharing days we both had similar high expectations about quality outputs. While we did not explicitly talk about this, we both instinctively knew we were striving to do the very best we could in our workplace.

You may wonder how we *knew* we had a shared work ethic. By the time we took on a job share together, we had worked in the same unit for some time. We had respect for each other's skills and abilities which had grown out of working together on joint projects. We had seen each other deliver quality work to budget within timeframes on a number of occasions. This is not to say we did the work in an identical way. In fact, we have different styles, sometimes work at a different pace and use different methods to get the job done. Yet we shared the overall goal of doing the best we could. Keeping our eye on this overall goal helped us merge our different styles into the best outcome we could produce.

Ability to share control

Feedback from our managers reinforced the view that the most effective job-sharing arrangements are those where accountability for outcomes is equally shared by both partners. This almost became our definition of job sharing.

We had to make shared accountability workable and, as we mentioned earlier, we did this by each taking a lead on particular projects. This required walking the delicate road of being aware of all projects, but intimately involved in some more than others and accepting full accountability for all of them.

Shared accountability becomes even more important where staff are involved. To ensure staff are not disadvantaged by the job-sharing arrangement, it is important that their managers speak with one voice. We developed this to a fine art over the years. This was evidenced by the fact that our managers could talk to either one of us and know that the other would be brought up to date. Our names almost became synonymous. There was a certain amount of ego that needed to be let go to be comfortable with this situation.

The most critical evidence of our joint accountability was a shared performance agreement. Our managers recognised through this agreement that we were both equally responsible for the outcomes expected from our unit. Performance evaluation, although conducted separately, recognised this joint accountability. The natural result was that we also needed to share any recognition for jobs well done.

A shared level of commitment to the arrangement

Entering into job sharing can make you feel very vulnerable. These feelings in part can be attributed to leaving the security of the familiar full-time environment and entering into an unknown, shared world where your career path falls out of the mainstream. It became very clear to us on a number of occasions that this was the case. We would bump into people, either as individuals or when we were together, and their first question would be 'Still in a job share?' as if our arrangement was not considered long term or mainstream. We think it is one of our achievements to this day that we were successful at job sharing over a long period of time.

Our shared level of commitment to the arrangement was evidenced in a number of ways. We worked hard to maintain the momentum of our job. This meant either tying off the loose ends of our work 'week'or, if this was not possible, we let the other person know what still had to be done. Making a call to the other, or dropping off important reading and having a comprehensive hand-over mechanism were the ways in which we supported each other and our working arrangement. We never used job sharing as an excuse to not deliver. In fact, we used it as a way to demonstrate the value we added to the organisation.

PERSONAL ATTRIBUTES

The types of attributes that make a good job-sharing partner are not dissimilar to those that you would look for in a business partner, or even a life partner! Some have even said that the level of negotiation involved in job sharing is greater than that involved in other partnerships. This makes the personal attributes of your partner particularly noteworthy.

Trust

A fundamental feature in successful partnerships is trust. The ability to trust or to be able to build a trusting relationship is the starting point. The trust is that we are both aiming for the same outcome and that while we may go about achieving that outcome differently, we trust that each will do the best they possibly can to achieve that outcome and in a way that will not deny the other's values.

The nature of the job-sharing relationship creates a certain vulnerability with respect to sharing responsibility and control. Your reputation to some extent is at the mercy of your partner. You need to be able to rely on that person to fulfil the obligations you take on as a partnership. This may mean going out of your way to keep the other informed, or handing over decision-making for a particular project, depending upon who is at work, and trusting the other to make the decision they feel is most appropriate at that time.

Flexibility

At the risk of stating the obvious, job-sharing partners need to be flexible. The very nature of the relationship epitomises flexibility. Often work cultures revolve around a full-time environment which rewards and recognises individuals more fully than teams or partnerships. Our work culture was no different. To choose to work in a shared part-time arrangement required not only flexibility in arranging our lives but also our mind-set. We approached our working lives with ideas and opinions that reflect different levels of clarity or certainty. Flexibility is needed when these ideas need to be joined into one.

In fact, we believe our flexibility has increased as a result of job sharing. This has had a positive impact on both our work and personal lives. We have learnt to approach situations in a much more open-minded way (see Mary's story below). In learning to be flexible, it has sometimes pushed us beyond our comfort zones. We have had to approach situations in ways that we would not normally do and in ways that are not our first preference. In moving through the zone of discomfort from time to time, our ability to deal with the unexpected and unknown has increased.

Mary's story follows.

I have learnt an enormous amount from our experience. Working with Angela has shown me the benefit of being open minded when working on projects. One of the funny things about us working together was the realisation that we think very differently.

Typically, I want to get in and do something and then alter things if they needed it on the way through. Angela typically wants to think things through from the beginning. You can imagine the sorts of interesting conversations we have had!

What is wonderful is that over time we actually could point out what the other was doing, and work at meeting each other's needs. I must say this approach resulted in some excellent outcomes. I think we also both learnt from each other and are much more rounded workers as a result. I know I feel better prepared to work collaboratively across all levels within our organisation.

Effective communication

The ability to communicate effectively can often be taken for granted or paid lip service; however, this becomes the linchpin upon which a good relationship can flourish. This is so not just in day-to-day personal relationships, but also in a job-sharing situation. One of the features of our arrangement, which was often applauded, was the seamless service we provided. We worked very hard to ensure we didn't present a disjointed approach to our managers or our staff. Naturally this didn't always work as well as we hoped, but we worked on improving the seamlessness through constant communication.

We organised our working week to facilitate effective communication. We ensured there was a cross-over day, where we were both in the workplace on the one day. This gave us a formal opportunity to debrief and handover. It also provided us with the opportunity to schedule meetings, discussions or workshops where we both needed to be present. This often made Wednesdays incredibly hectic! Despite this, there was an ongoing need for constant informal communication which usually occurred whenever our lives provided a window of opportunity. The constant communication ensured there were few, if any, glitches and built the bonds that kept the partnership together and successful. We cover some ideas for a good handover later in the next chapter.

Openness to feedback

As with many aspects of life, opportunities for growth present themselves when we are open to feedback. Working in a job-sharing arrangement provides an opportunity for a work colleague to observe and participate much more closely than in a normal work situation. Being open and honest and an effective communicator are key ingredients that become almost meaningless without being open to the lessons that can be gained from this type of working arrangement. Being open to feedback also means that continuous improvement in service delivery becomes second nature.

It becomes impossible to build the trust needed for a relationship to succeed without honesty. A job-sharing arrangement allows for a much closer working relationship than would normally develop in the workplace. You and your partner share insights into each other's strengths and weaknesses. The ability to share these insights honestly and constructively lays the foundations for a healthy and successful partnership. This provides a unique opportunity to grow professionally and personally.

In hindsight, we can confidently say that we each chose the right partner. We can say this because we worked together for over five years and in that time gained a deeper understanding of each other, both as work colleagues as well as people. In speaking to others in job-sharing roles it becomes clear that the work and personal attributes that we've touched on here are common to many successful arrangements and make a job-sharing proposition more likely to succeed.

Activity 9 provides a worksheet to use for discussion with a potential job-sharing partner. It will help you understand their skills and knowledge, work ethic, need for control, commitment level, trust ability and flexibility. You can compare these with your own to see if you complement each other.

■ THE JOB-SHARING PROPOSAL

A job-sharing proposal can be any way of putting your ideas down in writing and leaving them with your potential employer to consider. This may take the confrontation out of a face-to-face situation and give the employer time to think through your ideas and proposal. As we have stated previously, job sharing is out of mainstream. This means that it may not immediately seem as obviously a good idea to the employer as it is to the employees involved.

There are plenty of examples of putting a job-sharing proposal together on the net. Just type 'job share' into a search engine and you'll find plenty of reading material. A word of caution here, though. A crucial thing about job-sharing is matching it to the needs of your organisation. You need to think about whether a written proposal is the best way to go. Would a discussion be useful first? Or could you talk to your human resources area about arranging a presentation to key supervisors in your organisation from a consultancy group that specialises in flexible working arrangements? Think carefully about how to get the ball rolling and progress from there. For those who think that a written proposal would be the best route, Activity 10 also gives you some clues as to how to go about creating your own.

Just a few pointers to remember when completing your proposal:
• have at hand all the information you have collated from the previous activities and worksheets
• think about what will be important to your employer and write your proposal with that in mind — the benefits to be gained by the organisation

- if you refer to a particular person in your proposal check that this is okay with them
- ensure all your facts are correct
- be explicit about what you are proposing
- if anything in your proposal is likely to offend or put off any key stakeholders, do not use it.

■ AVENUES FOR FUTURE CHANGE

To ease the transition from full time to job sharing (and possibly back again), it may be useful to document the extent of the arrangement and any avenues for future change between the two partners. The job-sharing proposal would naturally become a key component of the agreement. This ensures the ground rules are clear up-front and that no one partner is left in a vulnerable position should the other partner decide to alter or terminate the arrangement. Activity 11 provides you an opportunity to create a job-sharing agreement which could form an attachment to your job-sharing proposal.

A job-sharing agreement could also include an annual (or some other appropriate time-frame) review of the partnership and its continuing or future direction. It may be appropriate to set up stocktake points to coincide with performance appraisal cycles. These become opportunities to record and celebrate achievements as well as ensure clear common ground for the next period.

This formalisation of the partnership can also be a useful tool for managers of job sharers. It may ease any uncertainty about the reliability of the partnership, clarify accountabilities and also address contingency plans for possible changes in the future.

■ SUMMARY

There does seem to be a lot of issues to work out before you start in a job share. Obviously you may not find time to consider all of the ones listed in this chapter. We do encourage you to think about a number of them. Our experience is that because job sharing is outside the parameters of 'mainstream', the more thought and planning that can be done beforehand the better. Working in a job share certainly is challenging. Some of you will find it easier than others, but in our experience it is worth persevering.

chapter 5

Put job sharing to work

- Communicating in the workplace

- Two bosses

- Keep an eye on your attitude

- Interacting within the organisation

- Sustainable strategies for success

The focus of this chapter is to provide some clues to help you sustain your job-sharing arrangement and thrive in your new found flexibility. Having done the 'hard yards' to find a partner, find or set up an opportunity, get organised and get started, you might think that's it. Like many other important things in life, our experience has shown us that to ensure your flexible work arrangements become a long-term success, you need to keep putting in an effort.

■ COMMUNICATING IN THE WORKPLACE

Relationships of one type or another are an integral part of most workplaces. They provide the glue that holds the different aspects of the job and the different parts of the organisation together. In a job share, these relationships are maintained by your job-sharing partner on the days you are not in the office. This can add another challenge to the daily routine. Maintaining relationships means having clear communication strategies/methods up and running.

SPEAKING WITH ONE VOICE

We cannot over-emphasise the importance of speaking with one voice. There are many examples of the need to do this in the workplace outside the job-sharing partnership. When a selection panel has to provide feedback to someone who has applied for a job, it has to speak with one voice otherwise the person who applied for the job may get confused. Often managers are asked to speak with one voice on behalf of the executive of the organisation.

So, speaking with one voice is commonplace, but to do it day in day out, keeping in mind at all times what your job-sharing partner may be thinking, is quite a different matter. It also involves a great deal of sensitivity and tact. We learnt this the hard way, on the job. By putting our experience to work as you set up your program you can circumvent much of that hard work.

One of the critical elements of speaking with one voice is regular contact with each other. In our experience, the 'handover' to each other was vital. The challenge was to determine how much context to give the other person and how much to leave out. We worked at this as we transferred information over the phone, in writing and face to face. At times we made this work by virtue of sheer will. We had to be patient with each other when one didn't readily understand what the other was saying. We worked at translating each other's body language and nuances into words, so that each person, although they may not have physically experienced what had happened, certainly understood it. We also tried to make the handovers fun — we knew we would have to spend time together, so we tried to enjoy it.

We found that speaking with one voice to our supervisor was generally easy — we just aimed to meet with him on the same day at the same time. If there were any important messages we wanted to give him or needed to hear together, we did just that. Obviously we had much more incidental contact with him as individuals, but by making sure the formal contact was together we allayed any possibility of confusion. When we met with our boss formally on a day when the other partner was not there, we made sure we conveyed the conversation and any decisions clearly to them.

We also worked hard at letting go of our ego — and found that there are many opportunities to do this in a job share! It wasn't unusual for us to be called by each other's names. After a while we learnt to laugh and shrug this off. It was just part and parcel of working closely together. By focusing on the outcome, we learnt not to hold onto personal ownership!

THE HANDOVER

With our performance inextricably linked through our job sharing, the transfer of information between us became crucial. We needed to be able to communicate clearly and in the shortest time possible. We agreed that it would make life easier for both of us to put in writing where we were up to with various projects. However, we needed to ensure this did not take as much time as doing the job! Our formal handover document evolved over time. This added clarity and structure to the transfer of information between us. As our job became more complex, this transfer of information became more and more important.

Over time our handover sheet became a more formal two-columned table with headings. The Projects column reflected those projects listed in our performance agreement and this in itself became a good reminder of the projects for which we were accountable. The Progress to Date column contained the details of the work itself and what the other person needed to know. We would each annotate the handover sheet towards the end of the work period or just add notes as important issues came up. In the end it all worked pretty well.

An example of our handover sheet follows. The actual content is not important, but it is worth noting the level of detail we put in in order to transfer information between us. This is only offered as an example of how we did it — it is important that any job-sharing partnership finds what works and is comfortable for them. There is no one single form or correct solution. Our handover sheet worked for us because we were able to divide our work up into projects — different types of work may require different types of solutions.

PROGRESS	PROGRESS TO DATE
PROJECT A	• I have cc mailed Geoff and Jenny re Thursday. The consultant suggested a 9.30 start. We already have another meeting on that day and it seems too good an opportunity to miss. I was wondering if it was possible to put consultant off until 10.30 and have the other meeting from 9.00 till 10.30.
PROJECT B	• We have got to a final (well close enough for the mock-up, we still need to work on the telephone numbers). A copy is on your desk. Market research advice is that we do not need to market test again. She has worked with me to deliver the draft. Her advice is that a portrait document will not help the readership of the document with our clients, she suggests we go back to the original concept. I think we get two mock-ups, what do you think? Please check that Lyall is getting both mock-ups done.
PROJECT C	• A copy is on your desk (only problem is that it is not in colour). We may get some feedback from the boss early on Monday. She is confident that all that needs to be in there is there — but just wants to step back and look at it from a wider perspective. • We agreed that we would try to get the final copy to the Board by the end of next week (she also mentioned that we could probably spill over into early the week after if we had to, but that we would aim for the end of next week). With this in mind we will try to get an up-to-date copy to her to take as reading on the plane to Adelaide (Tuesday night).
PROJECT D	• Susan is uncomfortable with the date of 17 July for the workshop. I asked her to nominate an alternative date and talk to Martin directly about this.
PROJECT I	• Gerard had Thursday and Friday off sick.
Other	• There is a workforce planning network meeting on 22 and 23 June. Jane will be using the network as the finance contact person in each branch. She is putting together an agenda and is wondering if you are available to talk to the group on strategic planning — business planning and our other key initiatives. I said I would check your availability. Please discuss with her.

Hints for handovers

In order to work out the salient features you will need in your handover document, you will need to determine the 'how' of your handover. Will it be verbal? Will it be verbal and written? Will you have any joint time in the workplace? And also the rules for 'what to include in a handover' and 'what to exclude in a handover'. For instance, what to include may look like:

- priority activities such as urgent tasks that need to be completed before the person leaving the workplace returns
- progress on ongoing projects
- latest sales figures that warrant joint attention
- issues you want written record of (important telephone calls, etc.).

What to exclude may be:
- less urgent tasks
- things that can be discussed verbally
- issues that need to be discussed verbally, such as stakeholder liaison (perhaps a written list could also be useful).

You will also need to have a discussion on how you would prioritise work. Check you are on the same wavelength. Talk over priorities in the handover.

If you use it, consider email carefully. Do you want all emails sent to one of you or automatically sent to both? How are you going to keep each other in the loop? Will you automatically copy each other in? How will you handle this for external clients? Also, how do you want to handle telephone calls that come in for a partner on the days they are not in the workplace? What language do you want used? For instance, 'Mary is not in the workplace today, however, we work closely together so can I help you?' is much more seamless than 'Mary is out swanning about in the sunshine today. Can I take a message?'

You can experiment, try things out on the job. But be patient and spend time getting the communication right. It could save a lot of effort and confusion.

■ TWO BOSSES

Supervising staff while working in a job share is a matter that needs to be carefully considered. It needs to be thought through from the staff's point of view and from your partner's point of view. We think there are two main ways of organising this supervision:
- having some staff reporting directly to one member of the job share and other staff reporting directly to the other member of the job share; or
- having staff report according to project — which means some staff members will report to both members of the job share, but on different projects.

We opted for the latter version (see the story below) which took some managing! We have had staff say to each of us, 'But [Angela/Mary] told me this when I was working for her on this project'. So it often took maturity from all parties, both of us and staff, to work our way through this issue. We also had to be very open to feedback and see where we may have given apparently conflicting guidance to our staff. Staff also had the opportunity to see how two supervisors managed using very different styles, as a result of our very different personalities. Over time, trust grew between our staff and us, and the situation clarified itself. However, it did take time and effort. Practical tools for feedback, such as 360-degree feedback (where formal anonymous feedback is received from subordinates, peers and supervisor), also helped.

Angela remembers one of our first experiences managing staff.

> *We were managing a small unit of staff who had never worked directly to two managers. They were having some difficulty in working with this new concept. In a conversation with one staff member, she made the comment, 'Your problem is that you are not like Mary'. Feeling naturally hurt and somewhat confused by this comment, I thought hard about what I could learn from it. I decided that I needed to raise it with Mary. When we analysed the situation and comment more closely we soon realised we needed to even more strongly communicate the needs of and responsibilities for staff and to ensure we provided a common management voice. In response, we adopted a lead project approach. Mary and I divided the projects between us as well as the staff allocated to each of these projects. Individually we took the lead on particular projects but continued to share overall responsibility for outcomes. This meant that the project staff involved had only one direct manager for each project.*

Having a joint performance agreement meant that we received both joint and individual feedback from our staff, peers and subordinates. This reflected the balance of being individuals yet being committed to joint outcomes. We have become pretty frank with each other over the years and both of us have found it necessary to relay good and negative feedback received from others to each other. Some people will even try to relay feedback through one partner of the job share to the other partner. When this has happened we tried to ensure that a direct line of communication exists. For instance, we would ask 'Have you two spoken to [Mary/Angela] directly about this?' To one another we would say '[So and so] mentioned this — you may like to follow it up directly with them'. Again this is the balance between maintaining direct relationships and having responsibilities for joint outcomes — the art of job sharing.

Comparisons are inevitable when job sharing. Mary has been told quite bluntly 'You are just not delivering to the same extent as Angela,' and Angela has been told in terms of her style 'Your biggest problem is Mary'. As you can imagine, comments like these certainly put pressure on the job-sharing relationship! However, with hindsight we handled things quite well. Accepting that comparisons are a fact of life, and that some people will simply 'click' better with one member of the job share as opposed to the other, it is just part and parcel of working closely together. This happens in a workplace where a team project is being undertaken. Some clients will find a person in the team that they relate to best and deal primarily with that person. The trick again is not to take it personally and simply get on with the job. So learn to take comparisons as part of the territory.

There are some advantages to job sharing in terms of comparisons. The biggest advantage is that one can learn from the other. Sharing ideas about how to manage a certain person, or what works when, or being clear about how to position each other in certain circumstances, opens up a wealth of possibilities that may not be possible when there is only one person doing the job. Don't overlook this important element — it can be a great opportunity for personal development.

SUPERVISING STAFF

People are sometimes shocked when they hear that we have supervised staff while working flexibly. One of the ways we found to deal with this is to work out how much time a person spends with their boss per week. This is an important point to ponder. Do staff need to be supervised all the time? If they do, are they the sort of people you want working for you anyway?

To be fair, if there are staff who are having performance difficulties this may require a different approach which does need fairly close supervision. We have had this circumstance occur more than once. One way around this was by having the under-performing worker report to someone else in the team, and then work with that supervisor to manage the under-performer. This can obviously work only in a multi-level team. Fortunately, this was the exception rather than the rule in our job-sharing supervision experience.

We did, however, learn as we went along and developed some approaches which improved the situation for both us and our staff. We found that the techniques or approaches did not necessarily need to be elaborate. For example, the discipline of regular team meetings with a regular agenda item would allow part-time supervisors on any issues to be updated and important information which they may have missed on the days that they were not at work to be shared. We made sure our regular team meetings were on a day and at a time when we were both in the workplace.

The following story outlines how a simple discipline Angela used helped her to manage her team.

As my working days are usually Monday to Wednesday, I set up a regular meeting with my team first thing Monday morning. This provided us with an opportunity to re-connect as individuals and as a team, discuss any important issues that may have arisen on the previous Thursday or Friday and to keep in touch with each other's work tasks and outcomes. Being very disciplined about holding short, sharp, regular team meetings helped everyone in the team feel that they were in touch. I've also had feedback in the past from my team that the meetings also provide a useful tracking device for how they're progressing on their projects. The meetings set the agenda for the week and are a useful way for staff to keep me 'in the loop'.

Another important lesson was learnt as a result of feedback from our staff. At one stage we underwent a formal 360-degree feedback process. One round of feedback provided very similar results for both of us, indicating that we were managing our peer and supervisor relationships very well, but had not been aware of the issues affecting staff. We were quite shocked by this. We felt we were working hard, so how could staff rate us, comparatively, so lowly?

When we were able to step back and think about what may be causing our staff to feel somewhat dissatisfied with our role as supervisors, it dawned on us that we were not sufficiently attuned to the impact our job-sharing arrangement may have been having on staff. We realised after discussion with staff that we were concentrating our energies on supporting each other first, then our manager, while our staff were coming a sad last. This was obviously not a conscious act on our part, rather it was driven by our strong commitment to purpose. Fortunately, having been made aware of this trap it then became relatively easy to meet the support and guidance needs of our staff. Some of the tools we discussed in both the previous chapters and this one may help you avoid falling into the same trap.

WORKING TO A JOB-SHARING MANAGER

We thought it important to share with you the reflections of one of our staff who worked to us.

A frustration or challenge was having to deal with two totally different people who thought very differently. I needed to make a switch to explain/deal with Mary or Angela. I realised that using the same technique did not work for each person, so I sometimes needed to find two ways to explain the same thing.

These two different ways of thinking helped me see that there wasn't just one way to do things. There isn't always a right way and senior managers don't always have the answers and sometimes need to work them out, just like everyone else. This was the biggest positive from the experience — there are different ways to achieve the same outcome. Mary and Angela brought different experiences and skills and I was able to get the best from both of them.

A key learning point for us was the awareness that, although we had done job sharing before, the team had no experience of it. In hindsight we could have taken more time to actively position the arrangement, for example, to explain why we were job sharing, how we work together, what to do if we seem to say different things, etc. This may have made the transition for us and the team much smoother. So you may like to save yourself some effort and keep this lesson in mind when you supervise staff in a job-sharing arrangement.

COMPROMISES

A question we are often asked is, 'Does working part time in a job share involve compromises?' It does. But then again, so do many other areas of life. The biggest compromise that we have had to make is letting go of control. (This does not mean letting go of all control and hoping that things will just work out.) The reality is that there will be times when you are simply not present in the workplace. There will be circumstances, events or announcements which will be missed. Our staff will continue with their work regardless. The working world will go on without us, quite nicely. In reality, full-time workers are unlikely to have total control anyway. So the real compromise here is letting go of the illusion of control.

■ KEEP AN EYE ON YOUR ATTITUDE

Now that you are on a roll with your job sharing or flexible work arrangement, there are a few things that you may wish to keep an 'active eye' over.

DON'T BE PART-TIME CENTRIC

We feel both grateful and fortunate to have worked for some time and to continue to work in flexible work arrangements, both job sharing and part time. We feel fortunate to have worked with organisations and employers who have had the foresight to be open to innovative approaches to work, allowing us to take time out to meet the needs of our families (such as caring for a young child or a sick parent) or for ourselves (to undertake full-time study). Flexible work choices can never be expected or demanded. They are merely options that may be available to meet the needs of individuals and organisations at different times of their lives.

Through our attitudes and behaviours, however, we can create and drive change in environments that enable and sustain flexibility. Because we consider flexible working arrangements to be more a privilege than an entitlement, we have taken responsibility to lessen the impact on others of this choice. We do this in a number of ways:

- by choosing to work in a job share — on most projects either job-sharing partner can talk about the work details whether the other is available or not
- through succession planning — we ensure we train others to do our jobs and take responsibility to steer and develop those who will eventually take over our roles in the future
- encouraging independence in staff — we encourage staff to use their own judgement wherever possible and use their expertise — if a supervisor is needed five days a week, eight hours a day, they may be over-managed.

We have worked in organisations where part-time and job-sharing opportunities are taken for granted and expected as an entitlement. The technical legalities of our employment conditions may vary but for us, flexible arrangements are something we work hard to preserve.

SHOW COMMITMENT

One of the key factors in our success as part-time workers has been the commitment we bring to the workplace. We touched on this briefly in the previous chapter but felt it was worth going into in greater detail here as it is commitment that at times will sustain the job share. Some of the issues that come up in relation to commitment include:

- having an active commitment to the work we undertake — this means going above and beyond the call of duty when necessary. Due to the choices we make in relation to the hours we work, it may mean finding extra time on non-work days or working longer on work days. Many senior managers do this. We try to manage this so that the extra hours do not become either high in volume or regularity
- part-time work does not mean part-time commitment — this is one of the comments some people have made to us and, as indicated previously, we respond with some passion to this suggestion. Ironically, we believe that *because* we are able to nurture our home lives our work lives take on more meaning and commitment, not less. Those who make 'part-time work, part-time commitment' comments are confusing time *at* work with commitment *to* work. They have a full-time mindset — that there is only one way to deliver in the workplace and that is full time. As you can see, we challenge this simply by the way we do our jobs.

DON'T BE A VICTIM

We had to overcome our own mindset in order to work flexibly in an effective way. We remember when we got our first round of 360-degree feedback. We discussed whether job sharing affected our results in any way. We recognised that job sharing was a possible dynamic in our feedback, but at the end of the day it was our individual results that were personally informative. We had to work at not using our work arrangement as an excuse for not addressing some of the leadership capability issues. The following short story from Mary gives some more detail about this.

I was working part-time hours as part of a job-sharing arrangement — my personal visibility in the workplace was part-time compared with others. A discussion with my boss showed me how easy it can be to use part-time as an excuse. I was speaking to him about my 360-degree feedback results, and we were also having a discussion about my performance rating (which resulted in performance pay). I think I said to him something like 'Well, being part time . . .' when he interrupted, looked at me squarely and said, 'Mary, I think you had better move on from being part time, I actually think it has nothing to do with your performance'.

Accepting this was very challenging for me. To be honest, I think I used my part-time hours in the job share as a bit of a security blanket. If I didn't succeed, I could always say it was because I worked less hours, or if I wasn't as good as my peers it was because I worked less hours. It took a lot of emotional honesty to realise I had made a clear choice about working part time and it was my responsibility to make my job a success — full stop. I had been carrying a real chip on my shoulder that was just an excuse. If life at work was unfair it was because I had chosen it to be that way (and who says life at work is fair anyway?). Overcoming this was the biggest step in being successful as a part timer, and in taking responsibility for my personal contribution to and the overall outcomes of our job-sharing arrangement.

ROLE MODELS

One of the hardest things about working flexibly (particularly job sharing) is that there are very few successful role models — both for men and for women. Perhaps the role models are hidden as they don't necessarily fit into the mainstream. Those of us attempting to work flexibly must remember that we are the role models for the next generation. This is hard work — and getting the balance between work and outside commitments can be difficult because most of the role models we have are those who are not working flexibly.

We must become our own role models with our own expectations and behaviours. This can be very personally challenging. Sometimes it is just a bonus to have someone understand and experience the world the way you do, as Mary's story below indicates.

I remember riding a lift with someone at work one day. I'm not sure how the conversation started, but somehow we got onto the fact that we were both working part time — I was in a job share and she was working reduced hours. There was an instant connection. We got out of the lift and stood talking in the foyer for ages. Our conversation moved rapidly through visibility in the workplace, the need to 'finish off' on the last working day, attitudes of co-workers, managing the boss and so on. Although my companion worked in the legal area of our organisation — an area unfamiliar to me — we had a lot in common. It was as if meeting someone with a similar work environment helped both of us feel supported and understood. I know for me, to hear my concerns echoed, my difficulties verbalised, to feel that connection with someone who experiences the workplace as I do, affirmed my experience and helped me keep my expectations realistic.

Undertaking flexible working arrangements means that there are very few role models. This is particularly so in job sharing, and even more so at a senior level. We did the best we could and learnt from experience — and there were many learnings on the way through. As you know, we believe that choosing a partner for job sharing is more of an art than a science. Well, actually doing the job is *both* an art and a science. The art is in managing the relationships and personal dynamics job sharing involves. The science is in the structure of getting the job done. Sharing the learnings about the art and science helps pave the way for such arrangements in the future.

■ INTERACTING WITHIN THE ORGANISATION

One of the key attitudes for successful part-time work is putting yourself in the shoes of others in the workplace. We have tried to do this in a number of ways:
- providing structure for those we work to and who work to us
- being flexible where possible and reasonable
- remembering what it is like to be full time.

We believe that job sharers, part timers and full timers need to work together to deliver effectively in the workplace. The workplace looses talent, experience and productivity if the only option is full-time work. Similarly, the workplace could not function effectively if job share and part-time work was the only option. It is the blending of personal goals and organisational goals that makes for a happy, productive workforce.

STRUCTURE YOUR INTERACTIONS

We have tried to apply the same structure as working full time when working part time. An example here is regular time with the boss. This is typically an hour, but it is formally reserved to discuss work issues. Obviously informal contact may occur in addition to this. As flexible workers we have found it very important to maintain the formal time as the informal opportunities are more infrequent. We will go out of our way to maintain the formal timeslot.

We also apply this structure to our staff. We have a regular meeting time — with some staff this is a formal time, and with others it is more 'ad hoc', but we have a commitment to check in with them once a week. All staff in our current organisation have a formal performance agreement which makes it easier to structure these discussions on a weekly basis. We find both the structured meeting time and the agreement on what the deliverables are for each project contribute to quality and build the bridge between working full and part time.

BE FLEXIBLE YOURSELF

We have touched on this a number of times and we do think it is important. Inevitably we have had to work around the needs of the workplace. One organisation we have worked for had a regular leadership program which required attendance interstate. However, approximately half the meetings over a two-year period were to be held on the days of the week not suitable to both of us. We appreciated that we were not the only ones with preferred times (others worked flexible hours too, or preferred travel on certain days). These leadership program dates were known well in advance so we planned our lives accordingly. So by considering the needs of the workplace and each other we were able to meet the needs of both.

A more straightforward example is when we wanted to schedule a time for a special team meeting with a social function at the end. The day that suited most of the workers was a Monday. This was not a handover day for us, so it meant that one of us would not normally be there. However, we both agreed that it was crucial that we were both present. So we arranged it — with a bit of give and take between our day care centre, husbands and friends, we both got to the meeting — and it was a turning point for our team. Without a little bit of give from one of us, the opportunity for great gains in the workplace would have been lost.

We recently came across another good example of flexibility from a part-time colleague who was required to go overseas on a business trip.

Robert works part time at a senior level. He has a high level of technical expertise and was offered a one-month trip overseas with his colleagues to visit a number of leading edge technological companies. This was no small acknowledgment of his talents. His first inclination was to decline because of the commitments in his personal life. However, discussions with spouse and family resulted in him recognising that this was an opportunity of a lifetime. So his wife took leave and all was arranged. The question here is, should his salary be increased while he was travelling overseas? He was now working full-time hours like everyone else on the trip. On the one hand he was delighted to have been considered suitable to undertake such a trip, but on the other he was wondering if he was eligible for an increase in salary. The issue of his salary was not raised by him or his employer. The question for flexible workers is, is this an issue?

REMEMBER THE FULL-TIME EXPERIENCE

We both had considerable full-time careers before we started working flexibly. In maximising the opportunities for flexible arrangements we think it is very important to remember what it is like to be full time. Most full-time workers will not have worked part time (or job shared for that matter) and have no idea what it is like, so it is up to all flexible workers (at least in the first instance) to make the effort and be understanding.

To be successful in flexible working arrangements we all must work to build a bridge of understanding between flexible and full-time work. Full timers have their own time pressures and responsibilities and we must remember not to be 'pushy' about getting what we want done, when we want it done. We need to respect each other's choices and move on from there. This requires maturity, flexibility and tolerance — qualities which exist in varying amounts throughout life and in the workplace!

■ SUSTAINABLE STRATEGIES FOR SUCCESS

This section is really about what we would have liked to do differently with the benefits of hindsight in terms of supporting ourselves. It is also about projecting forward what we would like to be better at in the future. We find that while it is relatively easy to talk about things that are important in supporting ourselves, translating this into action is another matter. We have come to the realisation that not prioritising or nurturing ourselves is okay only on a short-term basis. Over time, the failure to prioritise self-care can lead to a certain jaded burnout feeling — which can lead to cynicism born out of weariness. As with all the chapters in this book, please pick and choose what works best for you.

On the surface it may appear that someone who is working flexibly has already taken steps to reduce the amount of stress in their lives and so may not need to pay a lot of attention to self-support. However, we must admit that putting full effort into everything can mean at times that this feels very stressful, no matter what hours we are in paid work! However, our overall goal is to live a life spending more time enjoying life than being stressed about it.

OUR 7-POINT PLAN

We have developed a 7-point plan which we hope you will find useful in finding your own avenues for self-support. The seven points are:
1. be realistic
2. maintain self-esteem
3. let go of the job
4. strategies for sick family members
5. holidays and how to know when you need one
6. maintain professional development
7. support each other.

1. Be realistic

Balancing our expectations with what is realistically possible in our working week is something we have to manage carefully. It is very easy to try to take on more than is achievable and this in turn can lead very easily to burnout. The checks and balances we use which have helped us avoid burnout include:

- *Keeping an eye on what you agreed to.* We try to keep our jobs in perspective. We try to regularly step back and objectively consider the work we do in relation to what we agreed to do when we took on the job. Ideally this should all be covered in our regular performance appraisal and most of the time it is. However, if we think a discrepancy exists between what we do now and what we agreed to take on, then we may raise it with our supervisor — performance appraisal time or not. Alternatively we discuss it with a trusted mentor or friend.
- *Lead your staff.* Any supervisor needs to provide leadership to their staff. As a supervisor working in a job share you need to allow enough space in your job to do this effectively. The team you lead needs to be a realistic size for you to be able to do this. Determining this size is simply a judgement call and obviously will depend on the quality of the staff you have working to you. So when considering the job you are taking on or the work you are currently undertaking make sure you allow enough time for your leadership role.
- *Stay in touch with feelings.* Sometimes we find it important just to sit back and ask ourselves, 'On the whole am I enjoying this job?' Every job has its ups and downs, but how frequently we ask ourselves such a question and how frequently we answer in the negative can be a good guide as to whether the flexible arrangement is working. We have found that the enjoyment of our jobs has a big impact on how well we will do the job — so enjoyment and effectiveness go hand in glove. If we are regularly dissatisfied in the workplace, it may be that we either need a holiday, a new job or just to lighten up. Remember to talk it over with your job-sharing partner and allow time to do this.
- *Ask, 'What am I gaining and what am I losing by working flexibly?'* For instance, in our job-sharing arrangements we have gained time in our personal life, a very clear focus in our working lives and personal growth through negotiating and delivering on work outcomes in restricted timeframes. Compared to someone working full time we have lost money in terms of salary and, some would say, we have lost a fast track in our career path. It really depends on how you view it. However, a consideration of the pros and cons of your decision to work flexibly may help you determine if your expectations are realistic.

2. Maintain self-esteem

As a flexible worker it can be easy to feel as if you are living half a life at work and half a life elsewhere. On a bad day it can feel as if you haven't done anything well — it's as if you have left half the work *at* work undone, not paid enough attention to the other responsibilities in your life, not focused on your relationships and not had time for yourself. During times like these it is easy to let self-esteem suffer.

We know from experience that we each have our own strategies to help us through such difficult times. We also know that the easiest thing to do is ignore low self-esteem and to put off until later the issue of addressing it. This is not a way to sustain successful performance as a flexible worker. As self-esteem is such an individual thing we think it is important for each of us to find our own way of maintaining it, yet we still felt it important to share some of the things that have worked for us. Some practical steps we take to maintain our self-esteem include:

- catch yourself doing something you enjoy and start making a list of fun things to do
- ask yourself, 'Will it matter in ten years?'
- help someone
- gain some perspective by talking to someone in a different life circumstance
- think about self-nurturing — how do you nurture yourself?
  - eat well (as in healthy)
  - exercise
  - have a long chat on the phone to a good friend
  - have a facial
  - have a massage
  - read a book
- schedule nurture time into your diary and make it an immovable appointment
- get a week of early nights (or long nights) — when we had young children we remember going to bed for 12 hours to get seven hours sleep
- get a babysitter and spend some time with your partner
- ask your partner to babysit and have a meal with a friend
- do some reading on self-esteem — and find out for yourself what it is all about (Nathanial Branden is an expert in this area and he has written a number of books including *How to Raise Your Self-esteem*).

3. Let go of the job

Mentally letting go of the job on the days you are not physically in the workplace is a big challenge for someone who is job sharing — even though the job may well be someone else's responsibility for a few days! Letting go is a common experience for a number of people in the workplace, whether they work flexibly or not. However, we feel the issue may occur more frequently for flexible workers. The occasions that we have found easiest to let go of the job are when our lives outside work have been so absorbing that we have no choice (like writing this book for example). Nevertheless, in everyday life we have to manage ourselves so that work doesn't creep into every waking moment.

To counter this, we have found it important to have an 'anchoring' point which helps us move from one area of our lives to another. By this we mean some activity, some ritual, which helps mark the end of one activity in one area of our lives and the beginning of the next activity. We have spoken to a number of people about this and found that, like maintaining self-esteem, this is a very individual thing. Think about whether any of these strategies for letting go would work for you:

- having a shower and changing clothes when coming home from work (some people describe this as almost 'shedding a skin')
- doing exercise — on the way home from work if possible — like riding a bike
- coming in from work and having a drink to unwind
- mentally leaving pieces of work attached to the geographic landscape on the way home (for example, leaving this project on that billboard, or that task by that tree) and then mentally picking them up on the way back into work
- listening to loud music
- using a visualisation, imagine all the bits and pieces of work being tied up and drifting away on the last day of work, then just before you return to work, visualise all these images returning — some as solutions and some as ideas that have occurred while they were floating in the subconscious.

Of course there can always be the odd phone call in the middle of our non-working time that can pull us back into the job. We always try to make ourselves available for such calls because we figure a quick call now could resolve something and get it happening — whereas waiting a couple of days could really make things worse. Usually staff will only call when, by their judgement, there is no alternative. An answering machine can be really useful here. We will always get the message and can work on a solution before calling back.

4. Strategies for sick family members

Family members needing attention on working days is a challenge many working parents face. Having a back-up to your primary child carer is a must. We appreciate that this is not always easy. However, in terms of sustainability of a job-sharing arrangement and in terms of credibility, being in the workplace when you say you are going to be is very important. Looking after sick children is also important! Generally we have managed this by relying on our spouse and immediate family in emergencies.

We once had a colleague who managed this extremely well. With three children, a husband who worked full time and travelled regularly, this woman was the epitome of a flexible worker. Known for her professionalism, she was focused, pleasant and achieved a great deal in her working career. We were very interested in how she coped, particularly when her children were young. She told us how she became very good friends with another mother with young children who was also working flexibly. While the first port of call was husbands, these two friends would just not let each other down when it came to looking after each other's kids. Each knew that if the other called all other avenues had been tried. She laughed as she recalled the extent each would go to support the other — picking kids up from school, quarantining sick children from healthy ones and so on. We found it refreshing to hear this from someone who seemed so independent and competent, yet was able to reach out and receive support in a very collaborative way.

5. Holidays and how to know when you need one

Taking leave while working part time can be tricky. Not only will it affect your job-sharing partner, but you are already in the workplace less hours than most others — do you want to reduce this even further by taking leave as well? The reality is that job sharers need leave just as much as anyone else. Talking it through with your job-sharing partner well in advance, if possible, seemed to work well for us. We have come to the conclusion that there is no 'good' time to take leave, there is always *something* on the boil; however, there are obviously peak times or peak events when our presence is required. This is another example of personal goals matching organisational goals. We plan our leave, consider organisational requirements and just take it.

We find taking leave in this way is good practise at letting go of our job and encouraging staff to grow in their jobs. We recognise that all long-term job sharers need to relax and recharge to keep on top just as much as anyone else.

How can we tell when we need leave? It comes back to what we talked about in earlier chapters — self-knowledge and understanding feelings. Perhaps that little jaded, anxious or overwhelmed feeling that has been niggling. Perhaps it is a simple desire to inject some fun into our lives. One of the things we've struggled with is having enough leave in credit so that we can take it when we need it — this has particularly been the case after having taken extended leave to have children. One strategy is to keep a week or two in reserve. This means that if some emergency or event pops up there is the possibility of taking some leave.

6. Maintain professional development

Part of supporting yourself is not to neglect your professional development. This is a tricky one. Most weeks we are proud of ourselves just to have kept up with the regular demands of our jobs — but professional development? We find it very easy to let the excuses in here. Professional development, whether in the form of seminars, workshops, academic training or work placement, is great when working a full week in the office — although this can be hard enough to fit in. However, given the time such development can take out of an already shortened week, at times it just seems not worth the effort.

However, job sharing can put enough stresses on a career path without sacrificing development opportunities as well. Again, the creative solution must be sought. Some options we have taken up include:

- *Finding a course that begins on the weekend.* Although this can place more stress on family, on occasion we have found it a useful compromise between work and home. Some people think this is crazy — working on the weekend — and point out that this is very much contrary to achieving balance in one's life. However, we think as an occasional option it is a sound choice. We are very grateful for the opportunity to work flexibly, so if that means a fall back option is to work the weekend — so be it.

- *Making the opportunity for on-the-job training.* When working with contractors who are experts in the field, we have found it useful to factor in an extra day or half where the contractor briefs us (and some of our staff if appropriate) on their theory behind the contract deliverables. We have found this a very useful way of getting insight and understanding in the subject area we are working in.
- *Being highly selective about the courses attended.* We have found that attending a course can be done without too much compromise, particularly when the learnings or networkings will be useful in terms of day-to-day work. Sometimes we come back so motivated that the fact that we've been out of the office is readily forgotten.

7. Support each other

Whenever we meet someone who works flexibly we end up squeezing lots into whatever time we have together. We have had numerous conversations with people in lifts (and just outside the lift well where we have continued our conversations), in foyers of buildings, doctors' waiting rooms and all sorts of places. It just seems that we have so much to talk about and share. These conversations have reminded us how important it is for flexible workers to support each other. Our experience of flexible work (particularly in a job share) is not yet typical in the workplace, so not everyone will understand how we feel.

We have often discussed starting a support network for those working flexibly. The problem with flexible workers is that they are usually too busy to make the time to do something like this. The question we raise is whether we can actually afford not to. We believe it is important to maximise and build on the positive experiences of those working flexibly — the increasing casualisation of the workforce in the Western world is not a trend that will disappear readily.

One way to begin a support network, that is readily accessible and time efficient, is to do it electronically. A mailing list of flexible workers in your organisation is a starting point. A webpage or chat room for flexible workers is something else that could grow over time. These are quick and easy ways for tips, guest speakers, good books and latest success stories to be circulated among those who are interested. It only takes one or two to get things started. Suggested discussion topics could even be taken from this book.

A final word on mentors. This is a great way to gain support in the workplace. Job sharers need mentors as much as anyone else. We find being able to talk to and receive guidance from another is a good way of keeping perspective on our arrangement and our performance. As flexible workers we think it is important that we make ourselves available as mentors to others who are working flexibly. In some ways this is what we have tried to do in writing this book — to let others know that it is possible to make working flexibly successful.

So have a look around your workplace and among your friends and acquaintances to see if there is someone there who you could work with either as mentor or 'mentee'. It could be the choice that makes a real difference to your success as a flexible worker.

SUMMARY

We firmly believe job sharing is worth the effort. Look after what you've created and, above all, look after yourself. Good luck.

chapter 6

Activities

Purpose

To research the tangible and intangible elements of your organisation to determine how well a job-sharing arrangement may be received by management.

Resources

1. Official information relating to the employment conditions of your organisation. (This may be found on Intranet or Internet sites or from the human resources department.) The documents to look for include enterprise agreements (EA), recruitment policies (RP), information provided to staff on employment (SI), organisational values/mission statements (OV), business plans (BP).

2. Access to appropriate staff to observe, listen and question them on undocumented company policies/attitudes.

3. The worksheets below (you may wish to photocopy them if you are researching a number of organisations).

Steps

1. Use Worksheet 1 to record whether a tangible element is stated in official company documentation.

2. Determine the answers to the questions in Worksheet 2.

3. Using the information gathered in Steps 1 and 2, rate your organisation in terms of flexibility in Worksheet 3.

	OFFICIAL DOCUMENTATION					
	EA	RP	SI	OV	BP	OTHER

Is there provision for:
home-based work
teleworking
job sharing
flexible hours
access to single-day leave
parental/carer's leave
work-based child care
emergency child care places
school vacation care
financial support for child care
parents who may occasionally bring
    their child to work
work and parenting room
family friendly meeting times
paid care for out-of-hours meetings
    or training
spouse/child travel
Is the technology able to support:
job-sharing register
meetings without physical attendance
Are there extra provisions such as:
health and fitness assessment
on-site gym or fitness facilities
employee assistance programs
Other items please note:

_____
_____
_____
_____

Obviously, not all flexible organisations will have all these possibilities, but this checklist does give you an idea of what to look for.

How many staff are currently using flexible working options? _____

_____

Is it possible to speak to them to learn from their experiences? _____

_____

Is it possible to talk to a supervisor with a staff member who works flexibly to discuss the pros and cons of the arrangement? _____

_____

What sort of behaviour gets rewarded in the organisation? _____

_____

Does it relate to the number of hours worked? _____

_____

What do you know about the CEO's approach? _____

_____

Are they innovative? _____

_____

Do they encourage alternative approaches to achieving goals? _____

_____

What sort of staff do they attract to work for them? _____

_____

Do you see actual examples of the organisational values being lived out in the workplace? _____

_____

Do these examples reflect an organisation with a flexible approach? _____

_____

Tick the appropriate box as to how flexible/inflexible you rate your organisation. The rating system is from 1 to 5, with 1 being the most flexible and 5 being the least flexible.

	1	2	3	4	5
Open/closed	☐	☐	☐	☐	☐
Networked/traditional	☐	☐	☐	☐	☐
Empowering/autocratic	☐	☐	☐	☐	☐
Building/downsizing	☐	☐	☐	☐	☐
Relaxed/rigid	☐	☐	☐	☐	☐
Creative/tight	☐	☐	☐	☐	☐
Service focused/bottom line focused	☐	☐	☐	☐	☐
Synergistic/silo mentality	☐	☐	☐	☐	☐
Project based/task focused	☐	☐	☐	☐	☐

Using Worksheets 1, 2 and 3, work through the steps below.

Step 1

Look at your checklist of the tangible elements of the organisation (Worksheet 1). Is there enough evidence (ticks) for you to be confident that the organisation appears to support flexible work arrangements such as job sharing?

a) **Yes** — move to step 2.

b) **No** — check if you have missed any research. Think about whether you are prepared to consider presenting a job-sharing proposal which may be knocked back. Also consider that, if it is accepted, you will be trailblazing the way for others. This may sound a great adventure, but it may also involve extra effort. If you are prepared to give this a go, move to step 2. If not, you have a few more alternatives:

- Just wait. In your own mind and perhaps in others you may have raised the awareness of the potential of job sharing. Opportunities may present themselves at a later date.
- Give up on the idea for now.
- Look at other organisations that have tangible evidence of flexible work practices and consider changing employers.

c) **Not sure** — check to see if you have missed any research. Move to step 2.

Step 2

Consider your information on the intangible elements of the organisation (Worksheet 2). Are you satisfied at a gut level that the organisation would support job sharing?

a) **Yes** — you now have some building blocks for your job-sharing proposal.

b) **No** — if you are satisfied you have enough information you may need to consider your options. Undertaking job sharing in an unsupportive organisation can be hard work, and may be setting yourself up for failure. It may be a matter of time, or you may need to consider how you can still meet your goals in this workplace.

c) **Not sure** — you need to make a judgement call on whether you are prepared to put in the effort, if your proposal gets accepted, to make job sharing work in an environment which may not be supportive. This may mean convincing others as well as doing your job well. If you decide to go ahead you have some building blocks to support your job-sharing proposal.

activity 2 — Facing resistance to job sharing

Purpose

To prepare for some resistance to a job-sharing proposal.

Resources

Someone (whose opinion you value and who you trust) to role play a potential discussion with your boss — it could be a useful exercise to undertake this with your potential job-sharing partner if you have one.

Steps

1. One person takes on the role of boss who starts the discussion with the words in bold below.
2. The other person is requesting a job-sharing arrangement and they respond with their own words or some of the suggested responses.
3. Discuss the topic.
4. Suspend role play and discuss responses.
5. Resume the role play and move to the next topic.
6. Continue in this manner, adding new topics as they arise, until you have discussed all the pros and cons from both points of view.

Continuity in terms of customers is important to us

- Continuity doesn't always mean that the same person has to talk to the same customer.
- Currently when a particular staff member is ill the customer doesn't have to wait until the staff member is well before they get continuity.
- We are vulnerable if customer information rests with one particular person.
- We need to think about how we will cope if one person gets another job. We need insurance against this.

Timeliness is crucial

- The customer may not always need immediate contact. This may be inconvenient. What we need is a timeframe within which we will return contact to the customer.
- Face-to-face contact is costly and may be unnecessary. A telephone call may be just as effective and more efficient.
- We could divert the phone if the office is vacant.
- We have peak times when it is more important to offer this service eight hours a day, five days a week. This is not necessary all the time.

Job share costs too much

- There are more costs than pure salary/wages.
- We currently determine the cost of one worker in a number of ways — salary, accommodation, $ benefit to the business, etc.
- We currently determine productivity by considering a range of factors (*use the example here that best fits your business*).
- It would cost nothing to give it a go.
- One piece of equipment could be getting greater use over longer hours, in effect, at less cost.
- Two heads for the price of one!

Job share means double everything

- You are only paying for one piece of equipment, one phone, one desk.
- You could be getting double knowledge for the price of one.
- Double the benefits, half the cost.
- If you only wanted to pay for one of us to attend a particular training course, we could work that out between us.

activity 3   *Understanding yourself and your personal style*

Purpose

To help you know yourself better.

Resources

Any previous personality test (or similar) results which you may have taken. Access to the human resources section of your organisation, or a local community organisation offering self-development courses. The questions below.

Steps

Take some time to work through the following questions. These include some of life's big questions, so allow enough time — a week or even a month if you have it. Your answers may change over time as your self-awareness grows.

Understanding yourself

1. How well do you know yourself?

_____

_____

2. What do you want to do with your life?

_____

_____

3. Have you used any tools to find out more about yourself? If so, what did they tell you? If not, can you use the human resources section of your organisation (or someone in your local community) to help you gain more knowledge in this area?

_____

_____

4. How would you describe your values (again, your human resources section or your local community organisation may be able to help you articulate these)?

_____

_____

5. What situations cause you stress?

_____

_____

6. How do you cope with stress?

_____

_____

7. What are your strengths and weaknesses?

_____

_____

8. What sort of things keep you going when things get tough?

_____

_____

Your personal style

1. How would you describe your personal style?

_____

_____

2. If you had to draw a representation of your personal style, what would it look like?

_____

_____

3. Have you had feedback from others about your personal style? What did they say?

_____

_____

4. Have you modelled your personal style on that of someone else? Who? What was it you liked about them that made you want to emulate them?

_____

_____

5. Try to get some independent assessment on your personal style from your human resources section or local community organisation.

activity **4** *What are your motivations?*

Purpose

To help you work out what motivates you.

Resources

The questions below.

Steps

Use the questions below to categorise different aspects of your job.

(This activity is drawn from *Making Mentoring Happen* by Kathy Lacey.)

Find out what motivates you

Spend some time privately reflecting on the following questions or discuss them with your potential job-sharing partner or a trusted colleague.

1. Which parts of your current job are your main source of job satisfaction?

_____

_____

2. Which parts of your current job do you do well?

_____

_____

3. What is it about these tasks that causes you to like them?

_____

_____

4. Which parts do you like but do not do particularly well?

_____

_____

5. Which parts of your job do you not like but still manage to do well?

_____

_____

6. What causes you to do them well even if you don't like them? (In a job-sharing arrangement your partner may complement you here — they may like these types of tasks and be quite happy to do them, and vice versa.)

_____

_____

_____

7. Which parts of the job don't you like and don't do well?

_____

_____

8. What is it about these tasks that you do not do well? Why?

_____

_____

Passion Chart

Using the Passion Chart below, categorise your work tasks in four ways (the statements should help you do this):
1. things that you like and do well
2. things that you don't like, but do well
3. things that you like but don't do well
4. things that you don't like and don't do well.

LIKE	DON'T LIKE	
1.	2.	**DO WELL**
3.	4.	**DON'T DO WELL**

Reflect on where most of your work tasks fall. In a job-sharing arrangement it may be important to have tasks across all quadrants for both of you.

activity 5 Would flexible arrangements work for you?

Purpose
To help you think about flexible arrangements and whether you could try them.

Resources
The questions below.

Steps
Work through the questions below. If you are thinking about job sharing, share your answers with your potential partner (if you have one).

Find out if you are suited to working flexibly

1. Why do you work?

    _____

    _____

    _____

2. Do your work goals currently fit with your life goals?

    _____

    _____

    _____

3. How committed are you to these goals? What steps are you prepared to take to achieve them?

    _____

    _____

    _____

4. Are your life goals aligned with the implicit and explicit organisational values of your company?

    _____

    _____

    _____

5. Does your current job have clear work outcomes? Can these be achieved in a flexible work situation?

_____

_____

_____

6. What do you hope to gain by working flexibly?

_____

_____

_____

7. Is job sharing an option? On what basis are you making this decision?

_____

_____

_____

8. Is there anything you need to do differently to move to flexible work arrangements?

_____

_____

_____

9. How will you cope if work needs to be finished and you are out of the office for the next three days?

_____

_____

_____

10. Have you planned for the reduced income that working flexibly may bring?

_____

_____

_____

activity 6   *Positioning yourself in the workplace*

Purpose
To provoke your thinking about commitment, flexibility and priorities.

Resources
The activities below and some old magazines.

Steps
Work through the activities. If you are considering job sharing, you may wish to share your outcomes with your potential job-sharing partner.

1. Think about someone you know who you consider to be committed to their job. List how this is shown in their behaviour, attitude and energy.

    _____

    _____

    _____

    _____

    _____

2. Imagine a scenario where you are needed at work on a day when you don't usually work. List the alternative arrangements you may need to make.

    _____

    _____

    _____

    _____

3. Use pictures from old magazines to make a collage that reflects your priorities at this stage in your life. When you have finished, leave it for a few days, then come back to it and consider:
    *   how many priorities do I have in my life?
    *   what criteria did I use to determine these as my priorities (time spent, emotional energy invested)?
    *   are some more important than others?
    *   which of these priorities do I want to share in the workplace and what do I want to say about them?

activity 7 Remuneration checklist for flexible workers

Purpose

A checklist to help you negotiate remuneration for flexible working arrangements.

Resources

Checklist below.

Steps

Use the checklist when preparing for negotiations on remuneration. If you are considering job sharing, this is important to share with your potential job-sharing partner.

Checklist

Have you identified: Tick:

- the value you add to the organisation   ☐
- technical expertise   ☐
- years of experience   ☐
- professional profile   ☐
- past performance   ☐
- leadership qualities   ☐
- life experience   ☐
- the outcomes you have agreed to achieve   ☐
- how these outcomes will be measured and how transparent
  these outcomes are   ☐
- how often feedback will be given en route to these outcomes   ☐
- if you are in a job share, whether your remuneration will be
  considered individually or as a team   ☐

When determining remuneration, does your organisation consider:

- bonuses for flexible workers   ☐
- productivity levels of staff   ☐
- flexibility gained by not being in the workplace for a
  period of time   ☐
- any travel that may involve working more than the
  agreed hours   ☐

Purpose

To help clarify the best type of arrangement suited to you, your job-sharing partner and your organisation.

Resources

The questions below.

Steps

Consider the work you are proposing to undertake in a job share and answer these sets of questions.

Shared responsibility

	Yes	No
Does the work flow continuously?	☐	☐
Will you and your partner be able to communicate effectively across all parts of the job?	☐	☐
Is it feasible to co-ordinate the various aspects of the job between the two job sharers?	☐	☐

If you answered yes to most of these questions a 'shared responsibility' job share, where there is no division of duties, may be for you. Areas you may need to address with your partner include:

What strategies will you have to communicate effectively across all parts of the job?

_____

_____

_____

In which parts of your job do you just 'assume' effective communication (it is unlikely you will be able to communicate every piece of information to your partner) and how will you judge these?

_____

_____

_____

How will you manage staff?

_____

_____

What are the benefits to the organisation of having you work in this way?

_____

_____

Divided responsibility

Can the job be split into different aspects — by project or client group?

_____

_____

Do these aspects need a full-time presence or could they be managed in a part-time way?

_____

_____

Are there interconnecting parts within the various aspects?

_____

_____

If this is more the type of work you are looking at, a 'divided responsibility' job share may work well. Areas you may like to consider include:

Is one aspect likely to be more difficult or challenging than another aspect?

_____

_____

How will you determine this?

_____

_____

How will you determine who gets what part of the job?

_____

_____

How will you maintain best practice if you are working separately, yet in the same area?

_____

_____

Do you want a regular time to connect with your job-sharing partner?

_____

_____

What are the benefits to the organisation of having you work in this way?

_____

_____

Unrelated responsibility

Can the work be split totally separately?

_____

_____

Does this work split fall into less than, equal to or greater than one full-time job?

_____

_____

Are there clear benefits to splitting the work this way?

_____

_____

If this sounds more like you, an 'unrelated responsibility' job share, where the partners undertake completely different tasks, may be suitable. You may like to consider the following:

Is a connection with your job-sharing partner necessary?

_____

_____

What are the benefits of such a connection?

_____

_____

What can you learn from each other?

_____

_____

activity **9** *Personal and professional attributes*

Purpose

To help you and your potential partner discuss some of the attributes that may be necessary to make your job share a success.

Resources

The questions below and some time with your potential job-sharing partner.

Steps

1. Individually consider the questions below about personal and professional attributes. (We have listed them under the headings in the text.)
2. Share these with your job-sharing partner. (Note: you may not find it necessary to discuss all of these in detail.)
3. Where differences occur in your responses, consider how you will work with these differences.

Appropriate skills and knowledge

What are the skills and knowledge required to complete the job you are proposing to job share?

_____

_____

What are your personal strengths and weaknesses in relation to these skills and knowledge?

_____

_____

How will you know if your potential job-sharing partner has the technical skill and knowledge expertise to do the job?

_____

_____

_____

Consider how will you address any gaps.

_____

_____

A shared work ethic

Picture yourself living out your personal work ethic. What does this look like? For instance, does it mean:

- sitting back and reflecting before tackling a project and sorting out as much as possible before you start
- jumping in and learning by doing
- something totally different?

_____

_____

What personal development do you plan to take on in the first twelve months of the job?

_____

_____

Ability to share control

If your job-sharing partner had to make a key decision on a project you were both involved in when you were not in the office, what would you like to happen?

_____

_____

How will you feel if your job-sharing partner gets the credit for a job you did most of the work on?

_____

_____

What would you expect your job-sharing partner to do in this situation?

_____

_____

How will you feel if you are called by your job-sharing partner's name?

_____

A shared level of commitment to the arrangement

On a scale of one to ten, how would you describe your commitment to your job share?

_____

_____

What sort of work-related contact are you prepared to have when you are not at work?

_____

_____

Trust

What can I do to show you that I have a high level of trust in you?

_____

_____

What ongoing behaviours will continue to demonstrate this?

_____

_____

Flexibility

What does 'on time' mean for you?

_____

_____

Do you like to get a project completed well before time or put in a big effort just before the due date?

_____

_____

Communication

How will you know if your potential job-sharing partner has the relationship skills to do the job with you?

_____

_____

How will we communicate with each other?

_____

_____

How will we communicate with staff?

_____

_____

Openness to feedback

When I've got some feedback to give you — either positive or negative — how would you like it to be given?

_____

_____

activity 10 The job-sharing proposal

Purpose

To help you create a successful job-sharing proposal.

Resources

The worksheet below and some time with your job-sharing partner.

Steps

1. Determine the headings — purpose, background, proposal, costs, benefits, etc. — for your joint proposal. Just focus on the headings for now. Put yourself in the employer's shoes and think about what you would like to know.
2. Consider what needs to go under each heading.
3. Review your proposal and ask yourselves questions such as: What is an ideal length for this? Is the tone right? Have we covered all the bases?
4. Show your proposal to at least one other person that you both trust. Listen to their feedback and make appropriate adjustments.

You may wish to refer to the outline below as you develop your proposal. It provides some examples that may be useful. Remember to create a proposal that is right for you and your organisation.

Purpose

To outline a job-sharing proposal for the position of _____ [name of position] to be undertaken by _____ [your names]

Background

_____ [name of organisation] is committed to flexible working arrangements. _____ [your names] are looking for some flexibility in their work hours yet they are still committed to achieving at work.

OR

The nature of the work involved in the position of_____ [name of position] lends itself to flexible working arrangements. Discussions with the Area Manager indicate that a clear split of customers is possible. We are proposing an arrangement which allows a clear delineation of responsibilities for those customers who _____.

OR

_____ [name of organisation] considers itself to be at the leading edge of change. In the recent address by the CEO to senior staff, _____ [name of CEO] challenged us to 'Move out of our comfort zones and be prepared to try something different'. After hearing this talk, we decided to consider a job-sharing proposal.

Proposal

That the position currently known as _____ [name of position] be undertaken in a job-sharing arrangement, that is [spell out exactly what that means: shared, divided or unrelated responsibilities; how this work will be undertaken — split by customer group, region, project, etc.; who works what hours; how the management of outcomes will occur; will the arrangement be long term or short term, etc.].

Costs

[A budget for the overall costs]

ESTIMATED COSTS

	JOB-SHARE PARTNER A $	JOB-SHARE PARTNER B $
SALARY[1]	40 000	40 000
SALARY ON-COSTS[2]	40 000	40 000
ACCOMMODATION[3]	–	–
TRAVEL[4]	3000	3000
MOBILE PHONE	1000	1000
LAPTOP	5000	5000

1 Annual salary for this position is $67 000 per annum. It is assumed that a cross-over period is required and therefore is calculated by assuming salary for one full-time person is multiplied by 1.2.
2 Personnel on-costs such as insurance, leave entitlements, etc. are assumed to be 100% of salary.
3 Accommodation costs assume sharing one workpoint (i.e. desk, phone, computer, etc.). These costs are incorporated into broader organisational accommodation and are not factored individually.
4 In most situations requiring travel, this will be split most appropriately between two job-sharing partners.

Benefits

Open with a specific statement such as:

There has been discussion for some time about the benefits of splitting the northern customer region from the west and south-west regions. Potential benefits have been listed as improved customer relations, better product distribution and more concentrated new account management. Managing these customers through job sharing could result in the achievement of this split with minimal increase in resources.

OR

Our organisational goal is to maximise shareholders, return and to support our local community. For some time, part-time workers have contributed to this goal — their high productivity and quality of work are renowned. Coupled with the recent commitment by management to help staff with work and family responsibilities, we think that our proposal offers significant opportunity for our organisation. We suggest that the new production area be staffed by two people sharing one job. This would allow greater coverage of an extended work day, 5 days a week.

Other benefits include . . .

and then more generally say:

It has been shown that job satisfaction and output increase when flexible working arrangements are used. A survey of almost 200 people in senior jobs with flexible working arrangements, such as job sharing or reduced hours, found that 70 per cent had a 30 per cent higher level of output and scored higher on resilience, leadership and commitment than their traditional full-time colleagues. We believe that we would benefit from a job-sharing arrangement because it would allow us to integrate two key areas of our lives — our work and our family [or whatever] — without detriment to either.

Purpose

To help you create your joint job-sharing agreement.

Resources

The activity below and some time with your job-sharing partner.

Steps

1. List the practical details of your job-sharing arrangement. Some points you may like to document are:

- who is working when
- the time(s) you are both in the workplace
- your expectations around the workplace in terms of desk (one or two), telephone (one line or two)
- the title of the job you are planning to job share and key performance deliverables
- the length of time for the job-sharing arrangement
- benefits of the arrangement for the organisation.

2. List some of the less tangible elements of the job share, such as:

- the values you will operate under
- the reasons you wish to undertake a job-sharing arrangement
- what you hope to gain from such an arrangement.

3. Think about future avenues for change:

- how you would manage the circumstance if one partner wished to increase/decrease their hours
- the impact if one partner planned extended leave
- how much notice is reasonable if one partner wishes to terminate the arrangement.

4. Document your agreement. One approach is presented opposite. Create something that is right for you.

Job-sharing agreement

This job-sharing agreement is between _____ and _____
performing the position of _____for
the period _____ to _____working
[the hours and days of the week] _____.

We agree to meet regularly (e.g. every 2 months) to discuss key components of our job, such as:

- the job itself — reflecting on our agreed performance outcomes, resourcing levels and quality of our performance at work. We will provide evidence to support our discussion
- relationships within the job — such as those between supervisors, subordinates, peers, customers and each other!
- the job-sharing arrangement — time investment, what is working well and what we would like to change
- our personal challenges — whether we have achieved our personal goals, development needs and areas of greatest satisfaction.

Signed

X _____   Y _____

NOTES

1. *Work and Family*, August 2001, DEWR.
2. The Work and Family Awards are annually sponsored in Australia by the Work and Family Unit of the Federal Department of Employment and Workplace Relations (DEWR), AMP and the Council for Equal Opportunity Employment Ltd.
3. Finalists booklet for the ACCCI National Work and Family Awards 2001, DEWR.
4. ibid.
5. *Guardian* <www.guardian.co.uk/uk_news/story/0.3604.417507.00.html>.
6. <www.shlgroup.com/uk/news/SHLPressCuttings>.
7. Work and Family State of Play 1998, DEWR.
8. Work and Family Unit Job Sharing Fact Sheet, 1999, DEWR.
9. Russell, Graham, Bowmann Lindy, 2000, 'Current Thinking: Research and Practice', *Work and Family*, Department of Family and Community Services, Canberra, p. 9.
10. <www.ivilliage.co.uk>, 'What is job sharing?' by Clare Brennar.

REFERENCES

Albrecht, Karl, 1992, *The Only Thing that Matters*, HarperCollins, New York

Biggs, Susan and Fallon Horgan, Kerry, 1999, *Time On, Time Out!*, Allen & Unwin, Sydney

Bourke, Juliet, 2000, 'Corporate Women, Children, Careers and Workplace Culture', Industrial Relations Research Centre, University of New South Wales, Sydney

Branden, Nathanial, 1987, *How to Raise Your Self-Esteem*, Bantam, New York

Briggs-Myers, Isabel, 1993, *MBTI Introduction to Type*, 5th edition, Australian Psychological Press, Melbourne

Broderick, Elizabeth, 2000, presentation at the 'Listening to the Children' conference, Sydney

Covey, Stephen, 1989, *7 Habits of Highly Effective People*, The Business Library, Melbourne

Department of Workplace Relations and Small Business (DEWRSB), 1999, 'Work and Family State of Play 1998', Work and Family Unit, DEWRSB, Canberra

Department of Workplace Relations and Small Business (DEWRSB), 2001, *Work and Family*, Work and Family Unit (DEWRSB), Canberra, no. 26, August

Hall, Elizabeth, 1993, 'Job Sharing: Evidence from New Zealand', *Australian Journal of Management*, University of New South Wales Press, Sydney, vol. 18, no. 1, June

Handy, Charles, 2001, *The Elephant and the Flea*, Random House, Sydney

Lacey, Kathy, 1999, *Making Mentoring Happen*, Business and Professional Publishing, Sydney

McCallum, Ronald Clive, 1999, *Employer Controls Over Private Life*, University of New South Wales Press, Sydney

Margerison, Charles and McCann, Dick, 1990, *Team Management Profits Handbook: Questions and Answers*, Team Management Systems, Brisbane

Morehead, Alison, 2001, 'International Worklife Summit, London: A report', *Work and Family*, Work and Family Unit, Department of Workplace Relations and Small Business (DEWRSB), Canberra, no. 26, August

Morehead, Alison; Steele, Mairi; Alexander, Michael; Stephen, Kerry; Duffin, Linton, 1997 'Changes at Work: The 1995 Australian Workplace Industrial Relations Survey. A Summary of the Major Findings', Department of Workplace Relations and Small Business (DEWRSB), Canberra

Van Wijk, Gerry, 2001, 'Who's working part time?' Department of Workplace Relations and Small Business (DEWRSB), *Work and Family*, Work and Family Unit, Department of Workplace Relations and Small Business (DEWRSB), Canberra, no. 21, January

WEBSITES

<www.catalystwomen.org> Catalyst
Billed as 'the premier nonprofits research and advisory organisation working to advance women in business, with offices in New York, San Jose, and Toronto' this site does have a lot of interesting information for women in the workplace. They offer publications for sale and some free executive summaries of their research. It is well worth a look.

<www.flexexecutive.co.uk> Flexexecutive
Based in the United Kingdom, flexexecutive is a recruitment and consultancy service for individuals, businesses and schools interested in flexible working solutions. It is a comprehensive site relating to flexible working options and has specific information on job sharing, including a job-share register. Well worth a browse.

<www.geierlearning.com> Geier Learning Systems
Geier Learning is a renowned assessment performance company. Use this site to find out more about work attitudes and behaviours.

<www.ivillage.co.uk> iVillage
This is a UK-based website for women. It has some good pages that explain what job sharing is, how to assess if it is a worthwhile option for you, as well as your working rights explained.

<www.mommd.com> MomMD
A US-based website for women in medicine founded in 1999, MomMD is the first and only Internet community connecting mothers in medicine across the world. It has a job-share network and some interesting reading on job sharing in this profession.

<www.netmba.com> NetMBA
The Internet Center for Management and Business Administration site has an excellent summary of David McClelland's theory of needs. The specific reference is <www.netmba.com/mgmt/ob/motivation/mcclelland/>. Many university sites where human motivation is studied also carry good summaries of McClelland's work.

<www.pao.gov.ab.ca/health/flexible-work/jobshare> Government of Alberta
This site contains *The Job Share Guidebook for Employees and Supervisors* produced by the Personnel Administration Office of the Government of Alberta, Canada. It has some examples of job-share proposals, and covers some of the advantages and disadvantages of job share. It also provides useful insight on how this Canadian government handles flexible arrangements.

<www.womens-work.com> Womans Work: Flexible work for women
This US-based site is dedicated to helping women find professional flexible work. It has a range of articles and newsletters for working women and has a free job-share partner search and helps employers search for employees.

<www.workoptions.com> Work Options, Inc.
This is a flexible work advisory service run by Pat Katepoo who is widely acknowledged in the United States as a flexible work arrangement expert. The site lists a wide range of resources including flex success, strategies for approval, compressed work week, job sharing, telecommuting, part time and professional. A very useful 'how to' site.

<www.workplace.gov.au> Australian Government
This is the Department of Workplace Relations and Small Business (DEWRSB) website. It is worth a look, particularly under the Work and Family section. This includes a guide to part-time work and job sharing and much other useful information to those seeking to work flexibly. Aside from the quarterly *Work and Family* newsletter (with copies going back some years), this site provides a wealth of information for those managing life at work and life outside work.

INDEX